# Beethoven

# Beethoven

Martin Geck

translated by Anthea Bell
introduced by Peter Sheppard Skærved

HAUS PUBLISHING · LONDON

First published in German in the Rowohlts monographien series
© 1996, 2001 Rowohlt Taschenbuch Verlag GmbH

This English translation first published in Great Britain in 2003 by
Haus Publishing Limited
32 Store Street
London WC1E 7BS

English translation © Anthea Bell, 2003
Introduction © Peter Sheppard Skærved

The moral right of the authors has been asserted

A CIP catalogue record for this book
is available from the British Library

ISBN 1-904341-00-4 (paperback)
ISBN 1-904341-03-9 (hardback)

Designed and typeset in Albertina at Libanus Press, Marlborough

Printed and bound by Graphicom in Vicenza, Italy

Front cover: painting of Ludwig van Beethoven by Waldmuller
courtesy of Lebrecht Music Collection
Back cover: drawing by Carolsfeld courtesy of Lebrecht Music Collection

# Contents

# Introduction

No composer was ever more forcefully or rapidly established on the world stage than Beethoven. He achieved his rise to world fame, with apparently little effort, through the good fortune or effectively being 'composer in residence' to one of the first ever multilateral peace conferences. The myth of 'Beethoven', perhaps even the whole focus of western art music since, simply would not have happened without the Congress of Vienna in 1814–15, in which representatives of the nations of Europe came together to resolve the territorial disputes left by the Napoleonic Wars. The immediate international status which Beethoven acquired through his high profile at the Congress decisively shaped our understanding of the composer and the broad sweep of his work.

Beethoven's String Quartet Op 127 was premiered twice in Vienna in 1825. (The first performance, led by the great violinist Ignaz Schuppanzigh (1776–1830), was not successful, so a second, led by the young Josef Böhm (1795–1876), was arranged.) Within weeks, the same work was to be heard as far away as St Petersburg, in the suite of Prince Nikolas Galitzin (1794–1866), whom Beethoven had met when the Prince had been ambassador to Vienna. The St Petersburg performance was given by Beethoven specialists (by now spread all over Europe), including Bernhard Romberg, who had been with the young composer in the Electoral orchestra in Bonn.

Over the next decade in Paris the dominance of Beethoven's

oeuvre and personal philosophy transformed the consciousness of the listening public. By 1830, there were Parisian ensembles and societies specializing in the performance of his music directed by luminaries such as François Habeneck (1781–1849), Pierre Baillot (1771–1842) and Jean-Pierre Maurin (1822–94). In 1829 the young Hector Berlioz (1803–69) heard the late quartets in one of these early French performances; he was already modelling himself, both publicly and psychologically, on the musical and emotional image of Beethoven.

From the moment that his music was recognized in the German-speaking countries, Beethoven had considerable importance for British music and music making. The presence in England of such figures as his most distinguished pupil, the brilliant pianist and composer Ferdinand Ries (1784–1838), the publisher J B Cramer (1771–1858), the pianist and composer Muzio Clementi (1752–1832), and the impresario J P Salomon (1745–1815), ensured that the publication and performance of his music were of a high standard. The British saw him as somehow without nationalist allegiance or identity. This perhaps had less to do with his musical philosophy and his message of human brotherhood, than with his dishevelled figure – as portrayed in sketches of the time – striding around Vienna, hands clamped behind his back, wide-eyed, distracted, dirty and ferocious, which echoed the popular notion of the eccentric genius to be found in the poets of the day, such as Samuel Taylor Coleridge (1772–1834).

Tuning fork given by Beethoven to Bridgetower

The Manuscript catalogue at

the British Library includes the following entry, catalogue number Add.71148, an intriguing reminder of Beethoven's often under-estimated links with Britain, ranging from his arrangements of Scottish folksongs for the Scottish publisher and entrepreneur G S Thomson (1757–1851) to the commissioning of the Ninth Symphony by the Royal Philharmonic Society in London. It reads: ' Tuning fork said to have been given by Beethoven to G A P Bridgetower, with related documents, and a label in the hand of Gustav Holst.' Holst (1874–1934) actually in turn gave it to Ralph Vaughan Williams (1872–1958), and his widow gave it to the library.

There is no record of when Beethoven gave the tuning fork to the black virtuoso violinist, George Augustus Polgreen Bridgetower (1779–1860). The object itself might seem insignificant: a small elegantly crafted fork, slighter than most modern equivalents, nestling on a blue velvet cushion in a walnut box. The simple functionality of the gift somehow adds to its romance. Bridgetower, a British national, was of unknown African and Polish ancestry.

His father was personal page to Prince Nikolaus Esterházy (1765–1833). After a startling solo career as a boy, Bridgetower found himself working as solo violinist for George, the Prince Regent, later George IV (1762–1830), at the Brighton Pavilion. In 1802, he managed to persuade the Prince that he should travel to mainland Europe, to see his family, and also to meet with musicians in Vienna. George, in the aftermath of his father's 'mad-business', was commencing the building work

The violinist George Augustus Polgreen Bridgetower

that would transform the Pavilion into an Oriental palace. There was little point paying a musician to work in a building site and the Prince Regent was happy to provide his servant with an opportunity to improve his skills. For Bridgetower, this 'sabbatical' became the only way he could see of freeing himself from his service to the Prince. He certainly never showed any intention of coming back, so George's liberality failed to bring any greater lustre to his music room in Brighton. Bridgetower's trip had much in common with Beethoven's own journey from Bonn to Vienna in 1792. As Beethoven's patron in Bonn Count von Waldstein (1762–1823) put it, Beethoven was sent to Vienna on a training visit 'to receive the spirit of Mozart from the hands of Haydn' – and to bring it gloriously back to his employer's court. But, like Bridgetower, Beethoven never returned home.

The short, tempestuous relationship between Beethoven and Bridgetower resulted in the composition of the Sonata for Piano with Violin Op 47, now called the 'Kreutzer' Sonata. It was originally dedicated to Bridgetower. That much is clear from the dedication on the 'Forautograph' manuscript kept in the collection of the Beethovenhaus in Bonn. Little is known of the working relationship between the composer and the British violinist. The friendship ended almost as soon as it began, foundering, according to Bridgetower, because of a disagreement over a woman. Most likely their passionate temperaments were the cause of their parting. The 'Forautograph' was one of the few lasting relics of the relationship, along with some perfunctory letters from Beethoven to Bridgetower, the tuning fork, and Bridgetower's own description of a rehearsal of the sonata. This last document shows that the two actually played from the 'Forautograph' manuscript in rehearsal. The manuscript breaks off half way through the first movement, and is in Beethoven's sketchiest hand, as if written in some haste. Beethoven had to work up the sonata from his sketches for the first rehearsal. (This could be why he re-used the last movement of his earlier Sonata in A major Op 30 No 1, as the finale for this work.)

Tellingly, the manuscript does not include any of the cadenza material in the first movement as we have it today. The American writer Alexander Wheelock Thayer (1817–97), one of Beethoven's major nineteenth-century biographers, clarifies the working relationship that Beethoven had with the violinist. He describes a moment where Bridgetower imitated Beethoven's improvised piano cadenza, playing it spectacularly, an octave higher, racing into the stratosphere of the violin's range. Beethoven stopped, shocked, and then shouted 'Again!' this time holding the sustaining pedal of the piano down so that the violin was not left bare and unaccompanied as it flew up the C major arpeggio. This done, he leapt from the piano bench and embraced his colleague. This is a fantastic account of a player boldly stepping into the territory of the great composer-improviser, which for many people today, for Beethoven's colleagues and contemporaries, and even, to a degree, for Beethoven himself, was the privilege of his invention and imagination.

In common with all composers, before the time of Gioacchino Rossini (1792–1868) and Hector Berlioz, Beethoven's fame rested as much on his impact as a performer as on his compositions. To separate the professional virtuoso and improviser from the composer would have seemed perverse to Beethoven's contemporaries. Indeed, most of the laudatory accounts of Beethoven's playing, from his arrival in Vienna onwards, speak mainly of the impact of his extemporization, his extraordinary ability to evoke atmosphere and mood through improvisation, rather than his digital brilliance or subtlety or the merits of specific works. All players of the time – soloists, orchestra players or chamber specialists – elaborated existing works with cadenzas and ornamentation. This was the great age of the instrumental duel, fought 'to the death' between improvising soloists. Beethoven himself fought several such duels with pianists such as Abbé Joseph Gelinek (1758–1825), Joseph Wölffl (1772–1812) and Daniel Steibelt (1765–1823).

Beethoven's attitude to improvisation and ornamentation was revealingly inconsistent. He often shocked and even angered his colleagues by inserting unexpected and unwonted cadenzas into his chamber music, such as the Quintet for Wind and Piano Op 16. But he also remonstrated with junior colleagues and pupils such as Carl Czerny (1791–1857) and Ferdinand Ries (1747–1836) for taking precisely the same liberties that had brought him fame with the selfsame works. Looking at the first edition of the Sonata Op 47, one finds no violin cadenza where Bridgetower would have played it at the first performance. By the time the work was published their relationship had gone sour; Beethoven had changed the dedication to honour the French virtuoso and technical theorist Rodolphe Kreutzer (1766–1831), who in fact never performed the sonata. He was later to be seen running from a performance of Beethoven's Ninth Symphony with his hands over his ears.

Bridgetower shows us the great composer and his opinionated interpreter in collaboration and offers a tantalizing glimpse of the tempestuousness of Beethoven's creativity and compositional processes. Perhaps this was the only time that Beethoven worked with a string player whom he regarded as a peer, whether as a friend or artist. The dedication on the sonata is both affectionate and mocking: 'Sonata mulattica. Composta per il Mulatto Brischdauer – gran pazzo e compositore mulattico.' ('Mulatto Sonata. Composed for the Mulatto Brischdauer [sic] – great lunatic and mulatto composer.') The gift of the tuning fork seems equally ambiguous. It may have been a gift in the joshing spirit of their relationship: a helpful present, disguised as an insulting joke about violinists' intonation. Most likely, the two musicians were unable to agree on a standard pitch, which varied all across Europe and was invariably an issue when players from different countries sat down to work together. (It still is.) Perhaps they had an argument over the pitch of Beethoven's pianos, which we know, from the earliest accounts of his piano playing in Bonn onwards, he habitually mistreated and kept in wanton disrepair.

It would be typical of Beethoven to say thank you with such a backhanded compliment. He was always nastiest to his closest friends when trying to express affection. Perhaps Beethoven's knowledge of history might have provided a subtler agenda. It was the British inventor John Ford, one of Handel's assistants, who conceived the idea of the tuning fork in the second decade of the 18th century. If Beethoven knew this, his gift may also have been expressing his appreciation of the British contribution to musical technique and expression, from George Handel (1685–1759), Beethoven's stated favourite composer, and Ford, to Bridgetower and the Prince Regent.

To better understand Beethoven's environment, his friends, lovers, colleagues, and enemies, is to realize that he was very much of his time. Beethoven links the aesthetics of the Enlightenment to the revolution of popular Romanticism, whether expressed in politics or art. He also negotiated the shift from the age of patronage to the Industrial age.

Beethoven's struggle, his very human triumph over life's obstacles, is a common point of identification for listeners and performers. The idea of Beethoven has achieved significance out of all proportion to the man himself. Any performance that fails to live up to this ideal risks being perceived as contrary to this 'great spirit'.

No composer has been so deeply identified with music in its noblest form. Reading a biography of Beethoven both assists and hinders this identification. It depends on the reader's as much as the writer's point of view whether he or she is seeking a picture of a day-to-day Beethoven or a representation of superhuman greatness. It is difficult for anybody to write, think, or even play Beethoven. His music is part of all of us. To achieve an objective view of him would require us to step outside the collective sense of self that he helped to form. He has moulded our languages of expression, speech, taste, ethics, politics, love, and our every musical breath. In no composer before or since has the intimate grandeur of humanity found a greater unity.

PETER SHEPPARD SKÆRVED

The house of Beethoven's birth in the Bonngasse

'The spirit of Mozart from the hands of Haydn'

# Early years · 1770–1800

Ludwig van Beethoven was born in December 1770 into a family of musicians. The undisputed head of the family was his grandfather Ludwig the Elder (1712–73). Born the son of a master baker in 1712 in Mechelen, Flanders, Ludwig the Elder was already attending a choir school at the age of five, and embarked early on a career as a singer and choir-master. He was initially employed in this capacity in Louvain and Liège, and in 1733 went to Bonn as a member of the musical ensemble of the Elector of Cologne. There he eventually rose to the position of Court Kapellmeister. As a sideline, he also worked in the wine trade and as a moneylender. Ludwig and his wife Maria Josepha Poll had three children, only one of whom survived, Johann van Beethoven, born in Bonn in 1739 or 1740.

In 1767 Johann married Maria Magdalena Keverich (1746–87), who came from near Koblenz and was the daughter of a cook. Though only 21, she was already a widow. Her second marriage was, in some respects, hardly less

Electors were regional noblemen of the Holy Roman Empire of German Nations, so called because they were entitled to elect the Emperor. From 1198 until 1803 the Archbishop of Cologne belonged automatically to this illustrious circle. Initially merely an architectural term meaning 'small sacred room', the word Kapelle developed other meanings, denoting a 'sacred choir', then 'the whole body of musicians', and finally only the instrumental part of such an ensemble. The meaning of Kapellmeister followed a parallel journey, from being the master of the chapel to leader of its orchestra, and eventually the musical director. The Elector would have maintained his private Kapelle as part of his court.

unfortunate; at least, Beethoven's mother is credited with the comment: 'What is marriage but a little pleasure followed by a string of troubles?'[1] In her early years of marriage such views may have been the expression of an obviously melancholy nature. Later, Magdalena had other, more concrete reasons for complaint. Johann van Beethoven (1739/40–92) entered the electoral choir at the age of twelve and was engaged as a tenor in the Hofkapelle in Bonn when his voice broke. He made good progress in his profession at first. But as early as 1784 an official memorandum commented on him unfavourably, mentioning his poverty and 'a voice which is definitely deteriorating'.[2] By this time he was probably already an alcoholic. He had also been charged with attempted fraud, and later featured in an anonymous document listing 'good sleuths at present unemployed who can be hired cheap'.[3]

Maria Magdalena bore him seven children, of whom only their three sons Ludwig (1770–1827), Kaspar Karl (1774–1815) and Nikolaus Johann (1776–1848) reached adulthood. Ludwig, born in the parental home in the Bonngasse and baptized in the church of St Remigius on 17 December 1770, was their second child but since the first-born, Ludwig Maria, had lived for only a few days, the second Ludwig grew up in the role of eldest son and guardian to his brothers.

Beethoven's exact date of birth is uncertain. It is likely to have been 16 December , 1770. Beethoven himself obstinately maintained that his birth certificate fact belonged to his older brother, Ludwig Maria (who died in infancy). For most of his life he was convinced he was born in December 1772. In the 'Heiligenstädter Testament' he made himself out to be three to five years younger than he really was.

For some ten years after about 1775 the family lived in the house in the Rheingasse owned by the master baker Fischer. (The building, on the banks of the Rhine, was destroyed in 1944.) Fischer's children, Gottfried (1780–1864) and Cäcilie (1762–1845), were Beethoven's childhood companions.

According to Gottfried's memoirs of this period, Johann van Beethoven decided not to send his eldest son to Herr Ruppert's local primary school and instead 'sat him down at the keyboard early and kept him strictly at it'. Ludwig had to stand 'on a little bench' in order to play the piano; he also learned the violin and later the organ too. His father does not seem to have taken an indulgent view when, instead of studying systematically, the boy 'scraped away at silly, confused nonsense' on his instrument – when, in other words, he was experimenting and improvising.[4]

Ludwig must have discovered early that the sensations of happiness and power that can derive from the practice of music are accompanied by endless effort, distress, failure, and attacks on the musician. Artists growing up in such circumstances may come to regard their music as a kind of service; certainly, Beethoven later often talked of renunciation and responsibility. In a letter of December 1811 to Joseph von Varena he declared: 'My desire to serve poor suffering humanity in some way with my art has never, from my earliest childhood, given way to any other consideration.'[5]

Beethoven had even less regular schooling than other child prodigies. In arithmetic, he scarcely got beyond the hurdle of addition. Attempts at the simplest of sums are found on the adult composer's musical sketches; he had problems with the calculation and notation of musical time. It is both amusing and touching to read the lesson his nephew Karl gave his uncle a few months before Beethoven's death, testing him backwards and forwards on the multiplication tables from one to ten, and then noting: 'Multiplication is only a simplified kind of addition. The calculation is done in the same way. You write each partial product under its figure, and if it consists of two digits then the one on the left is added to the partial product of the next figure. Take a little example: 2348 multiplied by 2 . . .'[6]

SCHOOL

Gottfried Fischer describes his friend as: 'Short and stocky, broad-shouldered, short-necked, with a large head and round nose, his complexion deep brown, he always bent forward slightly as he walked.'[7] The young Beethoven was nicknamed 'Spangol', meaning Spagnuolo (Spaniard), because of his strikingly dark complexion. Though Fischer gives a vivid account of pranks and amusing scenes in the life of little Ludwig, he seems to have been something of a loner. One morning, when he had been gazing for some time out of his bedroom window, he apologized for his distractedness by saying: 'I was lost in such beautiful and profound thoughts that I couldn't let anything disturb me.'[8] Another story, in which Beethoven climbed up to the attic to look at the peaks of the Siebengebirge through a telescope, reinforces this image of introspection and romantic yearning.

We may doubt, however, whether Beethoven had much opportunity for such leisure. His career as a prodigy began early: even at the age of seven – and his father's advertisements claimed that he was a year younger – he appeared at a musical Academy in neighbouring Cologne, performing, according to the advertised programme, 'various keyboard concertos and trios'.[9] At the age of eleven, young Ludwig was performing with the Bonn Hofkapelle as unpaid deputy to the newly appointed organist Christian Gottlob Neefe (1748–98); at 13, after the court chamberlain and intendant of music Graf zu Salm und Reifferscheid had put in a good word for him (at first unsuccessfully), he became official deputy organist.

Beethoven's employer was Maximilian Friedrich von Königsegg, Elector and Archbishop of Cologne, who reigned from 1761 to 1784 and was also Prince Bishop of Münster. Maximilian Friedrich was a civilized and sophisticated ruler. 'The present government of the archbishopric of Cologne and bishopric of Münster is without compare the most enlightened and active of all the ecclesiastically governed German states. The ministry of the court at Bonn is made up of the most distinguished men,' wrote one travel writer in 1780.[10] Another account, dating from the same year, paints an unassuming backdrop to this administration: 'Bonn is a pretty, well-built city, and its streets tolerably well paved, all with black lava. It is situated in a plain beside the river. The Elector of Cologne's castle stands by the southern entrance. It has no architectural beauties, and is plain white in colour, without any kind of pretension.'[11] Although the Elector felt obliged to make economies after taking office, he was always a patron and lover of the arts. It was Maximilian Friedrich who had appointed Ludwig the Elder, Beethoven's grandfather, to the post of Kapellmeister, in the first year of his reign.

In accordance with the custom of the time, Bonn court musicians were expected to be active in three fields: church music, chamber music and the theatre. The church music of Bonn was dominated by the Italian style; the concerts, given mainly in the magnificent Akademiesaal of the Elector's castle, were widely praised and included, in Beethoven's time, an unusually wide repertoire of baroque and early classical music. The *Bönnisches Intelligenzblatt* wrote of the ceremonial for the inauguration of the university library in 1786: 'At mid-day there was a dinner at court, served at several tables, and in the evening, at half past five, a grand musical concert was given in the great Akademiesaal, attended by the great nobles and all the electoral councillors with their wives, as well as their grown sons and daughters, clergy, officers, members of the university, and almost all foreigners of distinction.'[12]

Elector Maximilian Friedrich did not maintain a theatrical company of his own, but gave financial backing to well-regarded private troupes, and latterly to a company managed by a husband and wife partnership, the Grossmanns. Plays were staged in a part of the castle known as the Comödienhaus, as well as, more frequently, *Singspiels* (semi-dramatised playlets combining dialogue and song), operettas, and occasionally more demanding operatic works. The general public had access to the standing-room area to watch these performances.

The young Beethoven took part in all this as organist, harpsichordist and – according to the salary records – also as a viola player, first acting as assistant to Neefe, the court organist, and then to an increasing extent taking on independent duties. He was thus exposed to many musically valuable influences, and was fortunate enough to be able to participate directly in all the major fields of court musical culture. He was also initiated into the particularities of court life. As a servant of the Elector, he was required to wear the kind of extravagant uniform that the French Revolution would soon sweep away. Gottfried Fischer describes his gala uniform as: 'Sea-green tail-coat, short green breeches with buckles, white or black silk stockings, shoes with black bows, white flowered silk waistcoat with flap pockets, chapeau, the waistcoat bordered with

The first known portrait: Beethoven in 1786. Silhouette by Joseph Neesen

real gold cord, hair worn in curls with a pigtail, cocked hat, sword worn under his left arm, with a silver belt.'[13]

Beethoven's home life was not so glorious. At an early age Beethoven and his brothers had to go to the tavern to find their drunken father and 'take him quietly home in the most tactful way, so as to spare expense'.[14] After his mother's death, in 1787 at the latest, Ludwig became the real head of the family. At the end of 1789 he petitioned the Elector to grant him half the salary that had been paid to his father Johann, who was now incapable of service, so that he himself could support his family. When Johann begged his son to keep this embarrassing fact secret, the traumatic reversal of roles was complete. Beethoven must have felt some contempt for Johann. Certainly, though his grandfather died on Christmas eve of 1773, when Beethoven was only three years old, it was Ludwig the Elder and not Johann whom Beethoven revered and took as his

Beethoven's revered grandfather Ludwig the Elder

example; he had Ludwig's portrait brought to Vienna in 1801, and hung it in a prominent position in his rooms.

His father was an important influence none the less, particularly for Ludwig's artistic career. Johann brought home persons of rank who could make a proper assessment of the boy's talent and who encouraged him to continue with composition. He also enlarged his son's horizons and introduced him to the educational possibilities of travel.

Of even greater importance was the welcome Beethoven found with the aristocratic von Breuning family of Bonn. In later life, he is said to have described its members as his 'guardian angels' of the time, valued particularly, no doubt, by a young man needing to escape his own family. Helene von Breuning, the widow of a senior court official, took a maternal interest in him; her daughter Eleonore (1771–1841), of Beethoven's age, was a friend in his youth; and her son Stephan (1774–1827), who went to Vienna in 1801 as a jurist, became a life-long friend. Many years later, in 1825 to 1827, as Beethoven lay dying, Stephan's son Gerhard (1813–92) was one

Christian Gottlob Neefe                    Johann Georg Albrechtsberger

Beethoven's extraordinary teachers

of the most regular visitors to his deathbed. Another such friend was the doctor Franz Gerhard Wegeler (1765–1848), later to be Eleonore von Breuning's husband, who in 1838 remembered that: 'Beethoven was soon being treated as one of the family; he not only passed most of the day here but often even spent the night. He felt free here, where he could move with ease. Everything combined to cheer his spirits and develop his mind.'[15]

It is hard to say now which of Beethoven's first music teachers, some of them known to us only by name, had any lasting influence on his career. One significant figure was the great violin teacher and pedagogue Franz Ries (1755–1846), who taught Beethoven alongside his friend Stephan von Breuning. These lessons, which, according to Gerhard von Breuning, centred on the *Études* of Fiorillo, were the beginning of Beethoven's deeply creative relationship with string instruments. But most important was Christian Gottlob Neefe, the court organist in Bonn and a capable and cultured teacher. Neefe, born in Chemnitz in 1748, spent the

Joseph Haydn                    Antonio Salieri

formative years of his training in Leipzig, where he encountered the works of Johann Sebastian Bach (1685–1750) and was inspired by the composer Johann Adam Hiller (1728–1804) to compose comic operas and '*Singspiele*'. At the suggestion of the Elector, an admirer of Mozart, he prepared arrangements and piano scores of Mozart's operas.

Neefe was convinced at an early stage of his pupil's genius. He taught Beethoven in the *basso continuo* tradition and used Bach's *Well-Tempered Clavier*, while at the same time introducing him to the music of Carl Philipp Emanuel Bach (1714–88), Haydn (1732–1809) and Mozart (1756–91). This was a remarkably up-to-date course of study, which prepared Beethoven perfectly for the demands of Vienna. Undoubtedly Neefe also encouraged Beethoven's interest in and sympathy for humanist and Enlightenment ideas. The credo of Neefe's autobiography of 1782 – 'I love the great men of this world if they are good men too ... I hate bad princes worse than bandits'[16] – has an echo in a remark by Beethoven written in 1793 for the friendship album of Johanna Theodora Vocke of Nuremberg: *Freedom is always to be loved above all else; the truth is never (even on the throne) to be denied.*[17] Beethoven may also have inherited from Neefe his belief in the special power of music.

In 1782 Neefe helped to get Beethoven's first published work printed (nine piano variations on a march by Ernst Christoph Dressler) and a year later wrote the first published comments on the young genius: 'Louis van Betthoven plays the piano with great facility and power, reads music from sight very well, and to sum up: for the most part he plays Sebastian Bach's *Well-Tempered Clavier*'[18] – an exceptional achievement for a 13-year-old boy.

The works that Beethoven composed during his training under Neefe are not generally ranked with the juvenilia of Mozart. This may have originated with their relegation to the end of the appendices of the catalogue, under the heading *Werke ohne Opuszahl* (Works without opus number). The three 1782–83 sonatas known as the *Kurfürstensonaten* (Electoral Sonatas) offer clear evidence of Beethoven's ability in his early teens. The three piano quartets written in 1785 already show Beethoven's strikingly individual expressive language, for all of their technical indebtedness to Mozart.

After 1785, Beethoven's productivity as a composer seems to have lapsed for a while. A brief period spent studying in Vienna, which began in the spring of 1787 but had to be cut short because of his mother's approaching death, does not seem to have had a major effect on his art, although Beethoven may have met Mozart in Vienna. (There is an appealing but doubtful story that Beethoven played for Mozart. When Mozart was unimpressed at Beethoven's first improvisation, Beethoven demanded a theme from Mozart to improvise upon. After hearing this, Mozart remarked: 'Watch out for him, he will have something to tell you.') It is possible that during these years, besides continuing his service at court,

Beethoven preferred to concentrate on his general education. At any rate, on 14 May 1789, aged 18, he registered for matriculation at Bonn University.

Unlike Haydn and Mozart, who learnt their musical trade as they performed and composed and had no opportunity to acquire a political and philosophical education, Beethoven evidently saw himself from an early stage as not only a rising composer, but also a man determined to take part in the general cultural discourse of the day. The musical philosophy he expressed in many of his works was not developed in isolation: scarcely any other composer drew on the intellectual springs of his time, from youth onwards, with such eagerness and determination. Later in life he was able to tell the publishers Breitkopf & Härtel, with some justification: *No treatise would be instantly too learned for me, although I make no claim at all to genuine scholarship, for I have endeavoured from childhood to understand the meaning of the better and the wise men of every age.*[19]

Living in Bonn and studying at its university, founded in 1786 by the new Elector Maximilan Franz (1756–1801, ruled from 1784–94), Beethoven was well placed to encounter the ideas of 'the better and the wise men'. The intellectual ferment of the city impressed the great linguist, philosopher and educational reformer Wilhelm von Humboldt (1767–1835), who remarked of Bonn that 'the best periodicals as well as learned and political journals and books' were to be found in the court library and even in 'the reading cabinet in the market-place'.[20] The atmosphere was liberal as well as intellectual. Schiller's *Die Räuber* (The Robbers) with its Robin Hood-like hero, which fell victim to the censors in many places, including Vienna, was staged in Bonn in the 1782–83 season soon after its première in Mannheim.[21] Elias van der Schüren, who was considered a freethinker, introduced the critical philosophy of Immanuel Kant (1724–1804) to Bonn University.

How much did Beethoven identify with these currents of

Friedrich Schiller (1759–1805) was, with Johann Wolfgang von Goethe, the most famous and influential German dramatist, poet and historian. As the main representative of the Romantic *Sturm und Drang* movement his early works concern the desire for political and individual freedom and other ideals of the Enlightenment.

thought? He admired Schiller's idealism enough to be already thinking, according to Schiller's friend Bartholomäus Ludwig Fischenich, of setting Schiller's 'Ode to Joy' to music in the early 1790s – something he would eventually do years later in the Ninth Symphony. Adding that Beethoven was 'all for the grand and sublime',[22] Fischenich suggests that there was to be more to it than a straightforward strophic setting of the poem (with a tune repeated for each verse, as in a hymn). Rather, the composer's idea, borrowed from Greek antiquity, was of a poetic and musical *Gesamtkunstwerk* (total artwork) of idealistic and humane value.

'Enlightenment is humanity's departure from its self-imposed immaturity. This immaturity is self-imposed when its cause is not lack of intelligence but failure of courage to think without someone else's guidance. Dare to know! That is the slogan of Enlightenment.'
IMMANUEL KANT, 1783

But the young composer was as much a pragmatist as a radical. Any musician of the time, struggling to make a living in a world of both aristocratic patronage and commercial music-making, would have had to be. He could also be an elitist and a snob.

Moreover, idealism and optimism that might seem remarkable now were then a part of the enlightened intellectual consensus. The thinkers of Beethoven's day were inspired by a sense of mission to lend their heads, hearts and hands to the cause of social and indeed human progress. In France, the passion of the Enlightenment and the successors of Rousseau, with his philosophy of equality and human nobility, fanned the flames of the Revolution; in Germany, concentrated trends of thought encouraged the philosophy and art of idealism. Together, these approaches added up to a rejection of the 'old' ways, the promotion of individuality and social and political freedom, and a belief in the readiness of adults to turn their abilities to the common good in a morally responsible manner.

'When France in wrath her giant limbs upreared / And with that oath which sounds air, earth and sea / Stamped her strong foot and said she would be free, / Bear witness for me, how I hoped and feared.'
SAMUEL TAYLOR COLERIDGE, 'France: An Ode' 1798

Beethoven was clearly inspired by the spirit of the time, and inspired it in his turn. But we must be wary of too easily seeing Beethoven the observer of his times in Beethoven the composer. The fact that the sounds of the French Revolution echo through his symphonies does not make the composer a Jacobin radical, and his attitude to Napoleon Bonaparte (1769–1821) was far too complex to be capable of direct expression in certain of his works. Beethoven's idea of 'absolute music' – music for its own sake – itself preclude any form of composition that expresses a direct political message or dogma.

Beethoven not only saw the

In 1922 the composer FERRUCCIO BUSONI wrote 'Liberté, égalité, fraternité: Beethoven is the product of 1793 [when the French king was executed and a revolutionary government declared] and the first great democrat of music. His aim: art should be serious, life joyful. His opus sounds ill-humoured because life is not joyful after all; in the spirit of a beautiful yearning for this fulfilment he rises up again and again against the suffering, wrathfully and rebelliously.'

FLAMES OF REVOLUTION

greatness of his age quite early; his age also saw the greatness of Beethoven. The 'enlightened' nobility entertained a low opinion of commoners, and hardly a better one of the educated middle classes, but they did value outstanding and brilliant individuals. Dreaming of a new intellectual aristocracy, they hoped to gain the necessary infusion of new blood by the adoption of great minds. Haydn's path to success was stoney and Mozart was more marvelled at than revered as a child prodigy, but Beethoven – though he was not spared the struggles of ordinary life – quickly donned the 'mantle of genius'.

Beethoven was aware of his place in musical history even before he left Bonn for Vienna at the age of 21. Count Ferdinand von Waldstein, a musically gifted member of the Bonn *Lesegesellschaft* (Literary Society), wrote in Beethoven's friendship album when the composer left Bonn: 'Dear Beethoven! You are now leaving for Vienna to fulfil your desires, which have been frustrated for so long. The genius of Mozart still mourns and laments the death of its charge. It has found refuge, but no employment, with the inexhaustible Haydn, through whom it longs to be united with someone again. Through your constant diligence, may you receive the spirit of Mozart spirit from the hands of Haydn.'[23]

It would be easy to underestimate the importance of these comments. It is now common to speak of a trinity of Haydn, Mozart and Beethoven, but to do so in the autumn of 1792 showed great perception. At the same time, Waldstein's words show the value by now ascribed to music by progressively minded people. Beethoven was not travelling to Vienna to complete his training with an eminent musical figure, as had perhaps been envisaged when he first visited the city five years earlier. To Waldstein at least, the aim was greater: no longer the acquisition of a 'musical trade', but the initiation of a musician into the 'spirit of music'.

The generation before Beethoven had paved the way for such

ideas. Waldstein was right to refer back to Mozart. Only now, however, could music finally be emancipated from the service of patrons and acquire its full dignity. To say so is, of course, only to describe a trend. The young composer who set off for Vienna in the autumn of 1792 did so supported by a stipend from an Elector who was no doubt less concerned with promoting the interests of a genius than with developing the skills of a member of his Hofkapelle, a man who would be at his service again after he had extended his artistic horizons. Maximilian Franz may even have chosen the appropriate teacher for Beethoven himself: Joseph Haydn.

By the time Beethoven went to Vienna in 1792 to study with him, Franz Joseph Haydn (1732–1809) was generally considered Europe's greatest living composer. Haydn wrote over a hundred symphonies, as well as string quartets, oratorios, masses and operas. Beethoven studied with him for two years. Though their relationship was uneasy (not least because Beethoven did not rank Haydn alongside Bach, Handel and Mozart), they never fell out completely.

In 1792 Haydn was shown Beethoven's Cantata for the 'Death of Joseph II', he immediately accepted him as a pupil. Beethoven left Bonn on 2 November. The journey was arduous and frightening, taking him across war zones and through lines of hostile troops. Eight days later, Beethoven arrived in Vienna and found accommodation at what is now number 30 Alsergasse – first in Wenzel Glaser's 'little attic room', then in apartments belonging to Prince Karl Lichnowsky (1756–1814). Lichnowsky frequently left his family estates in Silesia, then a part of Austria, to visit Vienna, where he maintained a string quartet. It was through Lichnowsky that Beethoven met the violinist Ignaz Schuppanzigh, who was to become one of his most faithful friends and collaborators. The prince, his senior by nine years, also gave Beethoven an *entrée* into the upper classes. Beethoven was not only to ornament Lichnowksy's musical afternoons and evening recitals as pianist and improviser and to write new compositions for his quartet, he

Ignaz Schuppanzigh (1776–1830). Violinist. He collaborated with Beethoven as duo partner, quartet leader, and concertmaster from the mid 1790s until Beethoven's death. Beethoven took violin lessons with him; his quartet, which at that time included the dedicatee of Haydn's cello concerti, Anton Kraft, was initially engaged at Prince Lichnowsky's palace. In its various manifestations, this quartet premiered all of Beethoven's String Quartets except the Op 131. Schuppanzigh was a well-known and popular figure in Vienna, famous as much for his weight problem as his playing, and the target of Beethoven's choral work 'Lob auf den Dicken' ('Praise to the Fat Man').

was also to be a friend – rather than a servant – with whom the Prince shared his apartments and even his meals. To Beethoven, who describes the Prince in a letter of 1801 as his *closest friend*[24] this was both an honour and a constraint. Beethoven is also quoted as saying: *Now I must be at home every day at half past three, change into better clothes, shave my beard and so forth – there's no bearing it!*[25]

In March 1794 the upheavals of war forced Elector Maximilian Franz to stop payment of Beethoven's salary, making the composer even more dependent on Lichnowsky's help. None the less, he was doing well enough to move into decent accommodation in what is today Löwelstrasse, behind the Minorite church, to hire a riding horse and engage a servant. From 1800 onwards Prince Lichnowsky guaranteed him an annual salary of 600 gulden.

At the end of 1792 Beethoven's father died, but Beethoven

maintained his links with his family and surrounded himself from the first with a coterie of Bonn friends. His brothers Kaspar Karl and Nikolaus Johann also moved to Vienna. Karl worked until his death on 15 November 1815 as a financial official in the state civil service, and sometimes acted as Beethoven's secretary; Johann began working as a pharmacist's assistant in Vienna, after 1808 had his own pharmacy in Linz and became increasingly prosperous. Beethoven's friends Franz Gerhard Wegeler and Stephan von Breuning also moved to Vienna and in 1801 he was able to repay his debt to his old violin teacher Franz Ries, leader of the Bonn court orchestra, when Ries sent his son Ferdinand to Vienna to take piano lessons from Beethoven.

An impressive circle of professional musicians and gifted amateurs formed quickly. It included, apart from Wegeler and Breuning, the violinist Wenzel Krumpholtz (1750–1817), the cellist Nikolaus Zmeskall von Domanovecz (1759–1833) and his almost exact contemporary Karl Amenda (1771–1836) who, after completing his theological studies and spending three years working as a violin teacher and soloist, was in Vienna during the years 1798–99, and first came to Beethoven's attention as an excellent string player. Their friendship continued by letter after Amenda's return to his native Kurland.

Little is known about Beethoven's relationships with women in these early years. According to tradition the singer Magdalena Willmann of Bonn rejected his proposal of marriage 'because he was so ugly, and half-crazed'.[26] This is probably an exaggeration. For one thing, though the quite numerous portraits of Beethoven in his early Viennese years may be generous – they usually show him with a fashionable 'Titus' hairstyle – they do not suggest an unattractive physical appearance.

However, Frau von Bernhard, a young amateur whose playing of Beethoven's works was attracting attention at the time, gives a similarly hostile verdict – and not just because of his looks: '[Beethoven] was small and insignificant, with an ugly red face covered with pock-marks. His hair was dark. His clothing was very ordinary and by no means of the elegance usual in those days, particularly in our circles. He also spoke in strong dialect and expressed himself in a rather common manner, nor did his nature show any outward signs of cultivation; instead, he was unmannerly in his entire conduct and bearing. He was very proud, and I have seen Princess Lichnowsky's mother, Countess Thun, on her knees before him as he lounged on the sofa, begging him to play something. But Beethoven would not consent.' [27]

Whatever his attractiveness to women, Beethoven's relations with the Viennese aristocracy were certainly unconventional. But it was precisely this unconventionality that made him appealing. Many of the younger Viennese nobility – with Lichnowsky leading the way – regarded Beethoven not as a mere salon attraction but as an artist. In the spirit of the age, they lionized him as a pioneering and powerful figure, even as their very own 'Bonaparte'. The 'wholly untamed nature'[28] that Goethe (1749–1832) saw in Beethoven in 1812 already seems to have fascinated them.

Beethoven's reputation as a piano virtuoso was quickly established, also he was performing regularly in Vienna from 1793. In 1795, he played his piano concertos in a concert given by the Viennese *Tonkünstlergesellschaft* (Musicians' Society) and in the same year visited Berlin, Dresden, Prague and Budapest, among other places, on a concert tour. As was then common, he participated in reputation-making (and -breaking) pianistic duels with his contemporaries. In 1799 he entered into a competition with the pianist Joseph Wölffl, a pupil of Mozart, and the following year pitted his skill against the pianist Daniel Steibelt in the house of the wealthy banker Count Moritz von Fries (1777–1826). According to the reminiscences of the Bohemian composer Johann Tomášek,

Steibelt performed a piano quintet of his own composition and then improvised on an operatic theme popular in Vienna at the time, on which Beethoven had written the variations of his Trio Op 11 shortly before. ' This aroused the ire of Beethoven's supporters and the composer himself. He now had to go to the piano to improvise. He went to the instrument in his usual and I might say rather ill-bred way, almost crashing down upon it, and snatching up the cello part of Steibelt's quintet in passing, placed it on the stand upside down (on purpose?), and picked out a theme with one finger from the first bars.'[29]

Beethoven was as dogged as he was mercurial, continuing his studies on his own initiative. The history of music has rarely known a composer who studied with more energy or stamina. Beethoven's zeal fitted the times: in this 'age of genius' there was no longer any fixed doctrine of music and composition. Art in the service of Progress could not stand still.

Beethoven soon discovered that even his lessons from Haydn were not enough. It did not help that the two do not seem to have got on with each other very easily, for all their acknowledgement of one another's qualities. At any rate, Beethoven was also studying behind the old master's back with the Singspiel composer Johann Schenk (1756–1836) and, on the recommendation of Haydn, continued to study counterpoint with Johann Georg Albrechtsberger (1736–1809), the highly respected music theorist. Since Albrechtsberger had just become Kapellmeister at the Cathedral of St Stephan in Vienna, he would also have introduced Beethoven to the composition of church music.

Beethoven also took lessons from Antonio Salieri (1750–1825) in the 'free style'[30] and more particularly in the composition of Italian song, and violin lessons from Schuppanzigh, which eventually metamorphosed into a vital workshop for the development of his composition. Later he approached the double bass player

Domenico Dragonetti (1763–1846) and the horn-player Johann Wenzel Stich (1748–1809) for information on the technical niceties of their instruments.

In 1795 Beethoven felt ready to present his Op 1: three piano trios dedicated to his teacher Haydn. He had already composed and published compositions, but he now resolved that his work should be ordered into a public record of his high artistic endeavour: every new composition was to be a milestone on the way to 'that which is noble and better'. So active an attempt to establish a canon and a narrative was a striking and telling innovation, even if in practice Beethoven was not wholly consistent. (He often gave the impression of a greater output of new works than actually existed by allowing publishers to assign new opus numbers to arrangements of existing works.) It took the forcefulness of a Beethoven to carry such a system through, and to have a certain degree of autonomy in dictating his own conditions to rival publishers. Beethoven's determination of his own, continuous series of opus numbers was commercially shrewd too. By facilitating the identification of specific works, it simplified negotiations with publishing houses and hindered piracy.

Beethoven's compositions were demanding. The piano-maker and teacher Andreas Streicher (1761–1833), a friend of Beethoven in Vienna, gave one of his young female pupils the Piano Sonatas Op 2 with the comment: 'These are new pieces which the ladies did not want to play, finding them too difficult and hard to understand.' But it would be wrong

Beethoven engraving by Johann Neidl c.1801

to overestimate the barriers to Beethoven's music. European cultural life around 1800 was remarkably sophisticated. Besides other genres there was room for *Bildungsmusik* ('improving music') which aimed to be a part of social discourse on a high level; it was demanding and complex, but at the same time it was intended to be generally comprehensible.

As the passions of Romanticism had their effect, this culture became looser and more relaxed. Few figures better epitomized and led this trend than Beethoven himself. In 1835 Robert Schumann (1810–56) wrote an essay devoted to the differences between the generation of Haydn and Mozart and that of Beethoven: 'Now and then a solemn wig might still be seen, but the bodies once so rigidly tight-laced were moving with much greater flexibility and grace. In comes the young Beethoven, breathless, awkward and distracted, hair untidy, chest and forehead bared like Hamlet's, an oddity arousing much amazement, but the ballroom was too cramped and tedious a place for him, he would rather stride out into the dark through thick and thin, snorting his disdain of fashion and ceremonial, while stepping around the flower in his path lest he crush it.'[31]

This is of course a Romantic image of the young Beethoven. But his first piano sonata published under an opus number – the Sonata in F minor Op 2 No 1 – does indeed fit Schumann's account very well, except that the first movement, in common with Beethoven's later writing, suggests not just the youth bursting breathlessly in but also a rich dialogue between emotion and structure, between passion and argument. This combination of the expressive and the structural – feeling and form – was to be a constituent feature of Beethoven's subsequent writing.

'Freedom and progress in the world of art'

# Years of fame · 1800–1815

## THE 'PUBLIC' BEETHOVEN

Beethoven was the first really successful freelance composer in the history of Western music. Before him, a musician who wanted to make a living from their profession had to choose between an appointment with a fixed salary, working as a private teacher, or a career as a virtuoso performer. It is true that Haydn and Mozart had achieved greater freedom than this, but the former only in retirement from his court post and the latter without conspicuous financial success. Beethoven, by contrast, was a successful freelancer at an early age, and despite the troubled times in which he lived, soon became famous throughout Central Europe. As early as 1803 a reviewer in the Leipzig musical periodical *Allgemeine Musikalische Zeitung* could write that he had 'long ago formed the opinion that in time Beethoven will bring about a revolution in music, just as Mozart did'.[32]

Initially it was as a composer for the piano that Beethoven set the tone in Vienna's 'musically highly cultivated' society.[33] A small drama of ordinary life offers a vivid picture of that musical culture. It must have taken place around 1803, and is reported by the composer's pupil Ferdinand Ries.

'Beethoven takes more trouble with me than I could have ever believed. Each week I receive three lessons, usually from ten o'clock to two or three pm. I can almost play his Sonata 'Pathétique', which might give you pleasure, because the precision that he demands is hard to imagine. To hear him improvise, however, may not be imagined at all – I have had this pleasure five times.'

FERDINAND RIES,
Vienna 6 May 1803

Beethoven was playing the early versions of what would later be the *Andante favori* WoO 57 for his friends Ries and Wenzel Krumpholtz. Full of enthusiasm, Ries immediately went to see Prince Lichnowsky, and for Lichnowsky's benefit tried to reconstruct the music he had just heard as faithfully as possible from memory. Delighted in his own turn, Lichnowsky got Ries to teach him some fragments of the *Andante* so that he could then play them when he visited Beethoven next day, with the jocular comment that 'he too had composed something which wasn't at all bad.'[34] Beethoven was infuriated.

If this anecdote is authentic it shows what a direct and intense interest those around Beethoven felt in his piano music and that Beethoven took nothing about his work lightly, even in small matters and with his friends. He was determined to control the fate of his compositions; free from unwanted interference. Mozart, always secure in his own self-image, might just have smiled. Beethoven, whose sense of self-worth derived mainly from his work, had to guard it rigorously at all times. Ries reports that he said of an inattentive man in the audience who was disturbing the performance: *I don't play for swine like that.*[35] On another occasion, Ries himself played a difficult cadenza in a performance of the Piano Concerto No 3 in C minor, though Beethoven had told him not to attempt it. Beethoven 'moved his chair violently' with indignation at first, but then, when Ries managed to perform the cadenza successfully, he electrified the audience by crying: 'Bravo!'[36]

Beethoven moved through the musical life of Vienna with casual confidence. George Bridgetower, a black British virtuoso violinist, wanted to introduce himself to the Viennese with a violin composition by Beethoven, but had to wait a frustratingly long time for it to be completed. When the composer did at last finish what would later be known as the 'Kreutzer' Sonata Op 47, there was no time to write out the parts separately; so Bridgetower had to play extempore from the original manuscript, while Beethoven played from nothing more than the sketch of the composition. (See the introduction for the full story.)

The art of the string quartet, raised to a very high level in the musical life of Vienna by Haydn and Mozart, acquired yet greater prestige there through the work of Beethoven. The results include the three compositions now known as the Razumovsky Quartets Op 59 of 1805–06, works where the combination of abstraction and passion represented a new peak of the genre, which moved Goethe to describe the quartet as 'four rational people conversing with each other'.[37] In 1808, when the Russian ambassador Count Razumovsky (1752–1836) became patron of Schuppanzigh's latest quartet, Beethoven, as the composer Ignaz Seyfried (1776–1841) remembered, was 'cock of the walk, so to speak: they tried out everything he composed hot from the pan . . .'[38]

'Cock of the walk' he may have been, but to establish himself as *the* composer of the new century and thus win over the wider public, Beethoven had to achieve symphonic honours. Against the background of such expectations, Beethoven held 'a great Musical Academy' – a concert organized by a composer or musician, at their own risk and for their own benefit – on 2 April 1800. We may see it as a particular mark of favour that Vienna's Burgtheater was made available to him for this purpose. The programme for this concert, the first public performance in Vienna for which he was solely responsible, was highly significant. It was normal on such occasions to court the public's favour with a motley programme containing many virtuoso pieces. Beethoven, however, aged not quite thirty, confined his programme to three names: Haydn, Mozart and Beethoven. Just when contemporary opinion was beginning to confer the status of classics on that triad of Viennese composers, Beethoven – like Napoleon – took the initiative and crowned himself.

The evening opened with a symphony by Mozart, who had died eight years earlier and was already a legend, but Beethoven's teacher Haydn, then at the height of his fame and greatly revered by the Viennese, was represented solely by two vocal numbers from *The Creation*, which had been known to the public for only a year and was thus a very new work. The concert organizer put himself at the centre of the programme: he improvised on the piano, conducted his Septet Op 20 and First Piano Concerto, and as the crowning touch concluded with his First Symphony in C, a symphony in the same key as Mozart's last, the 'Jupiter'. The 'spirit of music' was indeed being handed down.

Beethoven followed this first Academy with another in 1803 at Schikaneder's Theater an der Wien; this time the Second Symphony was on the programme, as well as the Third Piano Concerto in C minor, and the oratorio *Christus am Oelberge* (*Christ on the Mount of Olives*). But by the time the Third Symphony, the 'Eroica', was completed a year later, the traditional framework of an Academy was no longer suitable for its première. Musicians for an Academy performance were engaged and paid for a single evening and could not be expected or trusted to rehearse so difficult and extensive a work with the necessary concentration; the audience too might have felt overtaxed.

So Beethoven was happy to leave the rehearsals and initial performances of the 'Eroica' to the private orchestra of one of his leading patrons, Prince Franz Joseph Lobkowitz (1772–1816), reinforced by temporarily engaged musicians. Prince Louis Ferdinand of Prussia, himself a composer and a man whom Beethoven greatly admired, had the work performed at his Bohemian summer residence in Raudnitz in the autumn of 1804 and is said to have requested two repeat performances. This was exactly what Beethoven would have wished for: an indefatigable orchestra, courtesy of Prince Lobkowitz, together with an audience that was both enthusiastic and knowledgeable. The first performances in Vienna were similarly given at the semi-private domestic concerts arranged by the banker Würth and in the Palais Lobkowitz; only when the ground had been thus prepared did Beethoven venture on the first public performance, conducted by himself in April 1805 at the Theater an der Wien. Prince Lobkowitz could hardly have done more as a patron to Beethoven. In March 1807 he organized two subscription concerts at his palace; the programmes included Beethoven's Fourth Piano Concerto with the composer as soloist, the Fourth Symphony, and the overture to the tragedy *Coriolan*, all performed for the first time.

Beethoven's relationship with the Viennese public was not always easy. On 22 December 1808 he held another Academy of his own at the Theater an der Wien. The list of works performed before a public audience for the first time at this concert, which lasted four hours, is remarkable: besides the Aria *Ah perfido!* Op 65, written over a decade earlier, the programme included the Fifth Symphony, the Sixth 'Pastoral' Symphony, the Fourth Piano Concerto, the 'Choral Fantasia' Op 80, and parts of the Mass in C Op 86. Beethoven was unfortunately unable to make this extraordinary programme into a real public success: the court musicians were giving a benefit

'I felt like a man who expected to take a stroll through an inviting wood with a congenial friend, but who found instead only hostile entanglements, and finally emerged from the thicket exhausted and disheartened. Undeniably Herr van B. is going his own way, but what an eccentric, tortuous, way it is! Intellect, intellect, and more intellect, but without nature, without song! Indeed, there is nothing in the music but a mass of learning, without even a good way of conveying it. It is dry and uninteresting, a forced attempt at strange modulations and aversion to the conventional key relationships, a piling up of difficulty upon difficulty until one finally becomes impatient and loses all pleasure in the task . . . And yet, this music cannot be dismissed altogether. It has its value, especially as an exercise for already accomplished pianists.' A 1799 review of the Violin Sonatas Op 12 from *Allgemeine Musikalische Zeitung.*

concert at the Burgtheater on the same evening; the auditorium of the Theater an der Wien was bitterly cold; and the orchestra, assembled more or less at random, had scarcely had a chance to rehearse. The 'Choral Fantasia' suffered an embarrassing false start, as the orchestra did not know where to begin.

The fact that even Johann Friedrich Reichardt, a prominent composer and writer on music who appreciated and revered Beethoven and was present at this concert, was not immediately able to assess the significance of the two symphonies speaks for itself. Although he did praise the 'lively painting and brilliant ideas and figures' of the Sixth Symphony, the Fifth seemed to him simply 'too long'. For Beethoven, who, according to Reichardt, was already 'entertaining in his head and heart the notion that *everyone* here persecutes and despises him', the muted reception cannot even have come as a surprise; by now he expected little understanding of art from the 'jovial and good-natured Viennese'.[39]

Moreover, Vienna had no concert tradition of the kind that existed in London, Paris or Leipzig, and thus no obvious place for the performance of great symphonic music. As time went on Beethoven increasingly developed an attitude of mingled defiance and self-assurance: if these great creations were truly epochal works, they would make their own way independently of the approval or disapproval of the passing hour. It is perhaps significant that Beethoven did not choose to introduce the Fifth Piano Concerto to the public in Vienna, but gave the work its première at the Leipzig Gewandhaus in 1811.

To our present way of thinking, Beethoven's composing 'took off' in the first decade of the 19th century principally in the field of what would become 'absolute' music, that is to say the genres of the piano sonata, the string quartet and the symphony. But when we consider that at this time Mozart was remembered chiefly for his operas and *Requiem*, and one of the main reasons for Haydn's popularity lay in his two great oratorios, *The Creation* and *The Seasons*, it is evident that as a rule the general public responded more readily to stage music and church music. These genres involved action, dancing, texts, singing and ceremonial – everything to appeal to the layperson who finds purely instrumental music, with its higher degree of abstraction, more difficult to get to grips with.

It is true that Beethoven did not cater for every aspect of this market, but by the year 1808 he had produced a major work in each of these less abstract genres: a ballet, an oratorio, an opera and a mass. The music for Salvatore Vigano's ballet *Die Geschöpfe des Prometheus (The Creatures of Prometheus)*, which had its première in 1801, has been rather underestimated in terms of its contemporary importance and its place in the history of ideas. The myth of Prometheus, punished by Zeus for stealing fire from the gods, was extremely topical. As the bringer of light and benefactor of humanity, Prometheus was an icon of Enlightenment idealism, and, for many, a model or forebear of Napoleon Bonaparte. Vigano himself was not a ballet-master of the old style but a pioneer of the progressive dance style in which freer movement expressed emotion. There is no doubt that the many performances of this ballet at the Hofburg brought Beethoven more into the public eye than any of the one-off performances of any of his symphonies.

The Viennese collector of printed music Alois Fuchs tells us that Haydn greeted Beethoven in the street with the remark: '"Well, I heard your ballet yesterday, and liked it very much!" to which Beethoven replied: "Oh, dear Papa, that's very kind of you, but it is far from being a *Creation*!" Haydn, surprised and almost offended by this reply, said after a short pause: "That is true, it is not a *Creation*, and I hardly think that it ever will be" – whereupon they both, somewhat taken aback, took their leave of each other.'[40]

If this is only an apocryphal anecdote, it is nevertheless a good one; two years later Beethoven did try his hand at an oratorio, *Christus am Ölberge* (*Christ on the Mount of Olives*) Op 85. It was premiered in Vienna in April 1803. Criticism focused on its text, which was typical of the genre but felt to be old-fashioned. It successfully did the rounds of German oratorio societies over the following decades, but was valued less and less by the composer himself.

Now that Beethoven had achieved some success with this Passion oratorio, the director of the Theater an der Wien, Emanuel Schikaneder (1751–1812) – as well as a theatre manager, the author of, amongst others, the libretto for Mozart's *The Magic Flute* – thought it worth commissioning an opera from him. Beethoven moved into a kind of company apartment in the theatre building and began to write *Vestas Feuer* (*The Vestal Flame*), a 'grand heroic opera'. Dissatisfied with the libretto, he broke off composition after the first scene and turned instead to the story of *Leonore*, set in Seville, and telling of Leonore's attempt, disguised as a man, to rescue her husband from unjust imprisonment. The 'rescue opera' genre had become prominent in the wake of the French Revolution, particularly through the work of Luigi Cherubini, whom Beethoven admired, and his popular *Le Porteur d'eau* (*The Water Carrier*). Beethoven based his new opera on a German translation of *Léonore* by Cherubini's librettist Jean Nicolas Bouilly. *Leonore* was a work close to its composer's heart: married love conquers adversity, justice triumphs over despotism. It is possible that Beethoven conceived the opera with the idea of having it performed in the near future in Paris, home of the revolutionary ideal, and a place to which he felt strongly drawn at the time.

He was working on the score in the years 1804 to 1805; the première, delayed because of difficulties with the censor, took place on 20 November 1805. Against the composer's will it was given under the title of *Fidelio oder die eheliche Liebe* (*Fidelio*, or *Married Love*).

According to the *Allgemeine Musikalische Zeitung* it was 'received very coolly'[41] – one reason perhaps being that many of the distinguished persons who admired Beethoven had had to flee from Vienna as the French advanced to besiege the city. Next year, though Beethoven had very willingly produced a revised, tightened up version, the drama was given only two performances. This time, at least, the audience approved. After quarrelling with the theatrical director Peter von Braun, Beethoven demanded the return of his score. A piano score was published in 1810.

Liebig opera card scene from Fidelio

The composer had even less luck with his Mass in C Op 86, a work commissioned by Prince Nikolaus Esterházy, the grandson of Haydn's patron of the same name. Esterházy, who continued his grandfather's patronage of Haydn, had previously subscribed to Beethoven's Piano Trios Op 1. The traditional tale goes that at the première, given in 1807 in Eisenstadt, the Prince commented: 'My dear Beethoven, what have you done this time?'[42] Beethoven had to fight for some time to get the score published by Breitkopf & Härtel, but never doubted the value of his work, which Schubert is said to have greatly admired.[43]

In the autumn of 1809 the Burgtheater commissioned Beethoven to write incidental music for Goethe's tragedy *Egmont*. The composition included, as well as the well-known overture, nine more sung and instrumental numbers – including *Music descriptive of Clärchen's death* and a melodrama (music played under spoken words) to accompany Egmont's words, 'Sweet sleep'. Beethoven also had a great success at the beginning of 1812 with his incidental music to the festival plays *The Ruins of Athens* Op 113, and *King Stephen* Op 117 – works with texts written by August von Kotzebue, commissioned for the opening of the theatre in Pest (Budapest).

If Beethoven's standing, particularly in Vienna, suffered a slight setback during these years, the premières of the Seventh Symphony and *Wellingtons Sieg* (*Wellington's Victory or the Battle of Vittoria*; generally known as the *Battle Symphony*) Op 91 at the end of 1813 more than compensated. It was with these works that Beethoven stepped fully into the limelight and won the sympathy of all the Viennese. This was a time of national awakening for the European nations allied against Napoleon. In the winter of 1812–13 Bonaparte had had to withdraw from Russia, in June 1813 the Duke of Wellington had crushed the French troops at Vittoria in northern Spain, and the defeat of France had been sealed in October 1813 at the Battle of the Nations near Leipzig.

Although he still admired Napoleon, Beethoven shared in the widespread enthusiasm for his defeat. He composed the 'Battle Symphony' initially at the request of the inventor Johann Nepomuk Maelzel for his 'panharmonicon', a kind of mechanical orchestra, and then arranged it for a large, flesh and blood orchestra for two charity concerts on 8 and 12 December 1813. The wide public interest shown in this work, which was a great sensation, made it seem sensible to perform the Seventh Symphony, a work completed in 1812, on the same occasion.

In the generally euphoric mood, audiences received the 'Battle Symphony', in which Beethoven made the English army 'march' against the French, with particular enthusiasm. The orchestral forces deployed were enormous: some 70 string players, as well as a great deal of woodwind, four horns, four trumpets, three trombones, Turkish percussion, two rattles *to imitate the firing of rifles*, and *two large drums to give the effect of cannon shots.*[44] The Seventh Symphony also benefited from the general mood of rejoicing, since its finale can be interpreted as an expression of the ecstasies of victory. The audience demanded a repeat of the symphony's evocative *Allegretto*, which made 'a deep and enduring impression' on the composer and violinist Louis Spohr (1784–1859) – who was among those playing.[45]

The young son of Franz Xaver Glöggl, Kapellmeister of Linz, writes: 'On Sunday there was not a ticket left for the performance, and Beethoven allowed me to fetch him from his rooms at ten-thirty. He put his scores in the carriage. I could not talk to him during our drive there, for his mind was entirely bent on his compositions, and he kept indicating various tempos with his hand.'[46] He successfully conducted the performance himself, the court Kapellmeisters Antonio Salieri and Joseph Weigl (1766–1846) assisted him by conducting the cannonade, and such leading musicians as Louis Spohr, Giacomo Meyerbeer (1791–1864) and Johann Nepomuk Hummel (1778–1837) also participated.

In an address intended for the *Wiener Intelligenzblatt*, a Viennese newspaper, Beethoven, overjoyed and grateful, declared the musicians to be a *rare combination of outstanding artists, every one of whom, inspired by the idea of contributing something to the good of the Fatherland and observing no order of precedence even in subordinate positions, enthusiastically joined to create the fine performance of the whole.*[47]

The composer now ventured to hold another benefit concert of his own. It took place in the great Viennese Redoutensaal on 27 February 1814, and presented two successful works, the vocal trio 'Tremate, empi, tremate' ('Tremble, you ruthless, tremble') Op 116 and the Eighth Symphony, written shortly after the Seventh.

Beethoven was now at the peak of his public fame, and was so popular that in this year *Fidelio*, retrieved from oblivion at first out of a sense of sheer embarrassment, was a great success. At the première of this new version, heavily revised with the help of the violinist Franz Clement and other friends, there were 'stormy demands for the composer, who was greeted with enthusiasm' after only the first act.[48] Many further performances followed: the Viennese obviously liked to regard the opera's praise of liberty as a hymn of victory in the struggle against Napoleon, and wholeheartedly approved. Eight years after the failure of the opera at its original première, the reviewer in the Viennese theatre journal *Theaterzeitung* hailed the composer enthusiastically as 'a figure of rare stature in our trendsetting republic of the world of art' and praised the music of *Fidelio* as 'a deeply imagined, purely felt structure of the creative imagination, of the greatest originality, of the most divine elevation of what is earthly to the incomprehensibly divine'.[49]

Other vocal works, such as *Der glorreiche Augenblick* (*The glorious moment*) Op 136, '*Germania*' Wo94, and *Es ist vollbracht* (*It is accomplished*) Wo 97 written immediately before or during the Congress of Vienna of 1814–15 and referring directly to contemporary political events, added to Beethoven's fame if not to his stature as a composer. A benefit concert given in the great Redoutensaal on 25 December 1815 is like a last echo of the patriotic period that had gone before: the works performed included the setting of two poems by Goethe, 'Meeresstille und glückliche Fahrt' ('Calm Sea and Prosperous Voyage') Op 112, and the Overture (on the Name Day of the Emperor of Austria) Op 115.

Beethoven's rise as a freelance composer would not have been possible without the expansion of music publishing and the growing market for printed music. The composer published at first with the Viennese firms of Artaria and Kunst- und Industriekontor. But other publishers also approached him, expecting each of his new works to win public acclaim. Publishing houses would pay good and sometimes unusually high fees to have a work by Beethoven in the catalogue, although they did not agree to all the demands of the composer, who was now bent on commercial success. The highly-regarded Leipzig firm Breitkopf & Härtel, for example, declined to buy a series of works as an expensive set.

Not surprisingly, there were constant differences and mutual suspicion between Beethoven and his publishers over the course of time. For instance, a legal quarrel developed over the String Quintet Op 29: in defiance of all appearances, the composer doggedly refused to admit that he had sold the work several times over, thus indirectly undermining his own praiseworthy campaign for better protection of copyright. Today one can hardly reconstruct in detail the moves in the game as it was played by Beethoven and his brother Kaspar Karl, who sometimes acted for him. It is certain, however, that the composer was no little innocent.

Beethoven had a point when he told his friend the publisher Franz Anton Hoffmeister in 1801 that he had been forced into becoming *half a businessman*, for Vienna had no state publishing house such as that set up in Paris at the time of the French Revolution.[50] Around the same time, in conversation with 'a gentleman who was present', perhaps Georg August Griesinger, a friend of Haydn and the Viennese agent of Breitkopf & Härtel, he wished he had an exclusive contract which would free him from all commercial concerns: *I did not want . . . to neglect the work of composition. I believe Goethe has such a contract with Cotta, and if I am not mistaken, Handel's London publisher had a similar agreement with him.*[51]

When the gentleman objected that Beethoven was neither Goethe nor Handel, he was not pleased, and told Prince Lobkowitz, who was trying to make peace: *I cannot have dealings with those who do not believe in me because I am still unknown to the general public.*[52] This comment – only the rough gist of which has come down to us – may sound arrogant, but shows the strength of Beethoven's will to carve out a position appropriate to his talents. As early as 1809 he was receiving an annual pension, formally a private arrangement but in effect as if from the state of Austria, and provided by a triumvirate of his admirers consisting of Archduke Rudolph (1788–1831), Prince Lobkowitz and Prince Ferdinand Kinsky (1781–1812).

Beethoven himself seems to have drafted the terms of his 'contract' with his three noble patrons, which begins with the words: 'It must be the aim and endeavour of every true artist to obtain for himself a situation in which he can devote himself entirely to the composition of major works, and not be kept from doing so by other business or by economic considerations. A composer can therefore have no livelier wish than to devote himself undisturbed to the composition of such major works and present them to the public himself. He must also take thought for his old age, and try to ensure himself an adequate income.'[53]

'The daily proofs that Herr Ludwig van Beethoven gives of his extraordinary talents and genius as a musician and composer awake the desire that he surpass the greatest expectations that are justified by his past achievements . . . The undersigned have made the decision to place Herr L van B in a position where the most pressing circumstances shall not cause him embarrassment or impede his powerful genius.'
ARCHDUKE RUDOLPH, PRINCE LOBKOWITZ and PRINCE KINSKY to Beethoven, 1 March 1809

The spur for this arrangement was Jérôme Bonaparte, who had been installed by his brother Napoleon as king of Westphalia in northwest Germany and was trying to lure Beethoven to Kassel

Prince Karl Lichnowsky

Prince Franz Joseph Max von Lobkowitz

Beethoven's patrons in Vienna

to be director of his chamber music. It is doubtful that the composer was seriously considering this post or thought it suitable. Perhaps he simply wanted to find out what he was worth to the Viennese. As it turned out, they reacted with inducements to get him to stay in Vienna amounting to an act of homage. Beethoven was to receive 4000 Viennese gulden a year; even when they themselves suffered various financial setbacks, Archduke Rudolph and the Lobkowitz and Kinsky families continued to provide considerable sums. (It is notoriously difficult – and often misleading – to convert this into modern currency. But 4000 gulden a year, even allowing that later inflation reduced its value, was an extraordinarily generous

Archduke Rudolph of Austria (1788–1831), brother of the Emperor Franz, was a great admirer, friend, and patron of Beethoven. He played the solo piano part in the première of the 'Triple Concerto' at the age of 16. Beethoven's Mass in D Op 123 (*Missa Solemnis*) was composed for Rudolph's enthronement as Archbishop and Cardinal of Olmütz in 1820. Rudolph was himself a fine pianist and was taught composition by Beethoven.

Prince Ferdinand Kinsky          Archduke Rudolph of Austria

settlement. One calculation, from 1804, suggests that an average middle-class bachelor, could live comfortably in Vienna on 1200 gulden a year (even allowing for luxuries, entertainment and so on).[54] Representatives of these three donors paid Beethoven his pension every six months for the rest of his life.

There was another way in which the Viennese nobility acted as patrons; the subscription lists of many concert series read like a catalogue of the aristocrats living in Vienna.[55] Almost all Beethoven's compositions are dedicated to noblemen who paid a high fee to have sole use of the work for a few months – and who were sometimes kept waiting by the composer in spite of their substantial advances. Prince Lobkowitz, who was positively obsessed with Beethoven as an artist, almost exceeded his own financial means when he paid the composer 700 gulden and 80 gold ducats for the dedication and temporary rights to the 'Eroica' symphony and paid for a suitable performance of it. Prince Lichnowsky, on a journey to Leipzig, went as far as to negotiate personally with

FEES

the publisher Breitkopf & Härtel on Beethoven's behalf.

It is hard to say how far Beethoven could have relied on the bourgeois public of Vienna in these years, since that public depended largely on the patronage of the nobility to fund their culture. The concert life of Vienna was not yet very well developed, and from the first Beethoven composed less for the Viennese than for connoisseurs and musical amateurs from all over Europe. As early as 1803 the Parisian music journal *Correspondance des Amateurs Musiciens* mentioned piano virtuosi who would play only works by Haydn, Mozart and Beethoven. The First Symphony was performed, in swift succession, in Leipzig, Berlin, Breslau, Frankfurt am Main, Dresden, Brunswick, Munich and Paris.[56] Even the 'Eroica', regarded as an extremely difficult work, had performances in Vienna, Mannheim, Leipzig, Prague, Berlin, Paris and London within the first decade of its official first presentation.[57] Around 1815 Beethoven's symphonies, overtures and concertos could be heard in every European city of any size, and some of them in smaller towns too – not as a part of everyday musical life, of course, but as a special event.

### THE 'PRIVATE' BEETHOVEN

Although we know more about the life and work of Beethoven after around 1800 than of any earlier composer, it is difficult to find a consistent thread running through that life itself: it was put entirely to the service of his work, the myth of which has almost swallowed it up. A remark by Beethoven in 1823, expressing the composer's wariness of the ties of marriage, sounds like a more general comment as he looks back at the past: *Had I wished to devote my vital energies to such a kind of* [domestic] *life, what would have been left for that which is noble and better?*[58] Where progress in his art was not at stake, Beethoven was inclined to indifference.

A look at the various places where Beethoven lived illustrates the point well. From his fourth decade onwards he very seldom left the vicinity of Vienna, and then not for long. Around 1803–04 he seriously considered moving to Napoleon's Paris; King Jérôme Bonaparte, as mentioned above, offered him a position at his court in Kassel in 1809; and he was briefly tempted to go to England in 1825. But only his imagination was inspired by the prospect of these wider horizons; Vienna remained the fixed centre of his life. Yet

Beethoven in 1803. Miniature on ivory by Christian Horneman

within the city Beethoven was always moving around; he changed his lodgings in Vienna some 25 times in 35 years,[59] and seems to have taken instant flight from any hint of discomfort or discord.

His extant correspondence is of only limited use in the effort to trace the events of personal importance in his life. Mozart and Wagner (1813–83) go along with the tide of life in their letters, often polishing it up, of course, or deliberately adapting it for a particular correspondent, but still giving the reader a vivid insight into the vicissitudes of their lives and emotions. How vivid, for instance, is Wagner's account of his life as a young man starting out in his profession in Königsberg, starving in Paris, a revolutionary in Dresden, a refugee in Switzerland, an established artist in Bayreuth!

Not so with Beethoven. For one thing, personal letters have not been preserved with the same regularity from all phases of his life; for another, they give less information about the details of his situation than about his emotional state, pictured in grand, archetypal terms. The emotions Beethoven took seriously were not those he experienced directly at the time of writing, but the sense of his unalterable fate. It is this rather dramatic image of his life that we can trace, at least in outline, through the letters and notes – some of them very personal – that survive.

From our present knowledge of the sources, it seems that the theologian and violinist Karl Amenda was one of the first to whom Beethoven wrote about his 'fate'. At the beginning of 1801 he told his friend to expect *a long letter from me about my present circumstances*, and confesses in advance: *It is certain that while two people had all my love, and one of them is still living, you are the third – my thoughts of you can never be extinguished.*[60]

On 1 July 1801 a long letter was indeed sent to Kurland. *Your B. is living a very unhappy life, . . . you must know that the most precious thing I have, my hearing, is much impaired; I already felt it when you were still with me and said nothing, but now it is getting worse and worse.* If he had his *full faculty of hearing*, so Beethoven continues, he would visit Amenda. However: *. . . my best years will fly past without my achieving all that my talent and powers bade me do – I must resort to sad resignation; although I have resolved to overcome all this, how is that possible? Yes, Amenda, if my disorder proves incurable in six months' time, you leave everything and come to me, for then I shall go on my travels (it is in my playing and composition that my disorder still affects me least, but it is worst in society), and you must be my companion.*

Two days earlier, Beethoven had told his other friend who was *still living*, Franz Gerhard Wegeler, of his despair at the continued weakness of his hearing: *. . . my ears keep buzzing and humming day and night; I can say that I pass my life wretchedly, and for almost 2 years have avoided all society because I find it impossible to tell people I am deaf. If I were in any other line of work it would be easier, but it is a terrible affliction in my profession, and as for my enemies, of whom I have quite a number, what would they say?* Beethoven next expounds his philosophy: *. . . I have* *often cursed the Creator and my existence, but Plutarch has shown me the way to resignation. If it be possible I will defy my fate, although there will be moments in my life when I am the most miserable of God's creatures.*[61]

Another letter to Wegeler, of 16 November 1801, is in similar vein: *The buzzing and humming is a little fainter than usual, particularly in my left ear, which is where the disorder really began, but my hearing is certainly in no way improved.* The fact that Beethoven was once again *mixing more with society,* as he writes in the same letter, was the work of *a dear, enchanting girl who loves me and whom I love; for the first time in two years I have some moments of happiness again, and it is the first time I have felt that – to marry could make me happy, although alas, she is not of my station in life – and now indeed I could not marry – I must be always on the move, but for my hearing I would have travelled half the world over by now, and so indeed I must.* He will not give up, he writes: *I will grasp Fate by the throat, it shall not bring me down entirely.*[62]

With these three letters, Beethoven was paving the way for the document known as the Heiligenstadt Testament, written on 6 October 1802, but only found amongst his papers after his death.

Karl Ferdinand Amenda and Franz Gerhard Wegeler, members of Beethovens' intimate circle.

It begins with the words: *For my brothers Carl and . . . Beethoven. Ah, you men who take me for a surly, refractory or misanthropic soul, or say so of me, what an injustice you do me! You do not know the secret reason for what makes it seem thus. From childhood my heart and mind were disposed to the tender sense of goodwill, I always wished to do great things, but remember that for six years I have been prey to an incurable condition made even worse by useless doctors, hoping from year to year for some improvement but always disappointed, and at last obliged to face the prospect of a malady of long duration (to cure it may perhaps take years or even be impossible). Born with an ardent, lively temperament and even inclined to enjoy the pleasures of society, I had to withdraw into seclusion early and pass my life alone, and if from time to time I wished to ignore all that then oh, how harshly was I repulsed by the doubly sad experience of my poor hearing.*

Beethoven describes the *humiliation* he suffered *when someone stood beside me, hearing a flute played in the distance, and I heard nothing*, and continues: *Such events drove me close to despair; it wanted but little and I would have put an end to my own life – only my art held me back, for it seemed to me impossible to leave the world before I had done all that I felt called upon to do, and so I endured this wretched life – truly wretched; I have so sensitive a physical frame that a rather swift change can cast me from the best condition into the worst – patience – so they say, I must choose as my guide, and I have – I keep hoping that my determination will hold, to endure until it pleases the pitiless Parcae* [the Roman goddesses of fate, one of whom drew out the thread of life] *to break my thread, perhaps I shall improve, perhaps not; I am determined – forced even in my 28th year to be a philosopher, which is not easy, and harder for the artist than for anyone else – Deity, you look down on my inmost soul; you know it, you know that it is inhabited by love for my fellow men and a desire to act well – O humanity, if you should ever read this, then think that you have done me an injustice.*

As if writing a genuine will, Beethoven turns in the following lines to his brothers Kaspar Karl and Nikolaus Johann (whose name, as in the salutation, is left as a blank space) as his heirs, to Prince

Lichnowsky and to his doctor Julius Adolph Schmidt. He asks his brothers to recommend to their children the path of virtue, which alone can bring happiness: *I speak from experience, it was virtue that raised me out of misery myself, and I owe it to virtue as well as to my art that I did not end my life by suicide.* Beethoven, as he finally remarks, will make haste towards death *boldly* and *with joy: . . . should it come before I have an opportunity to develop my capacity for art to the full, it will come to me too early in spite of my*

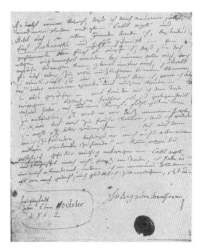

The last page of the Heiligenstadt Testament

*harsh fate, and I shall doubtless wish it to come later – but even then I shall be content, for will it not free me from endless suffering?*

In a postscript written on 10 October Beethoven also takes leave of Heiligenstadt – a village near Vienna where he felt he was in particular harmony with nature. The *fine summer days* for which, on medical advice, he had gone there had now passed away like *the autumn leaves* – and with them the *high courage* which had always inspired him before. Finally he sighs: *O Providence – let one pure day of joy come to me – my heart has been a stranger so long to the echo of true joy – when, when, O Deity, can I feel it again in the temple of nature and humanity? Never? – no – ah, that would be too hard.*[63]

The fact that at around the same time Beethoven wrote a brisk letter to his publishers Breitkopf & Härtel, among other matters praising the *really entirely new style* of the Piano Variations Op 34 and Op 35 and endeavouring to cast the right light on his importance as a composer in other ways,[64] suggests that the Heiligenstadt Testament should not be regarded as a spontaneous reflection of his current state of mind. Rather, the composer, summing up his life and shaping what was undoubtedly the real pressure of the suffering he felt at the time, produces something more like a work of literature, modelled perhaps on Goethe's seminal novella of youthful despondency and suicide, *The Sorrows of Young Werther*. For all their forcefulness, the words are carefully chosen; only the postscript conveys a note of immediacy.[65]

Was this 'testament' really intended for a certain set of people – for instance his brothers? Nikolaus Johann would no doubt have been displeased to see his name consistently omitted, whatever the reason for it. When Beethoven charges his brothers, still unmarried at the time, to bring up any children they may have in the path of virtue, it sounds more like a general didactic remark. Beethoven probably had in mind not so much his brothers and friends as humanity at large, whom he addresses in the opening words *O you men*. Humanity in general entirely misunderstands him in considering him a *surly, refractory or misanthropic soul,* when he is really a man of tender feelings, goodwill, a lively temperament, a sociable nature, a strong love for humanity and great moral conviction.

Subliminally, the Heiligenstadt Testament is a cry for love, security, warmth, and cheerful social intercourse with the rest of mankind. But Beethoven does not express the lack of these things directly. Instead, he translates it immediately into a moral struggle. Humanity has no insight into the hard fate that afflicts him, and so cannot help or understand him. The composer must rise above his experience of deprivation, becoming a philosopher, a stoic, and thus a moral victor. To avoid further risk of disappointment, he withdraws. Beethoven is not quite actually lowering himself into the grave – willingly abandoning his earthly existence – but he is renouncing all claims on life. Henceforth it will have only one meaning for him: to provide space in which he can develop his *capacity for art to the full*. As the great Beethoven scholar Maynard

Solomon writes, the Heiligenstadt Testament is a 'daydream compounded of heroism, death and rebirth.'[66]

In his letters to Amenda and Wegeler and in the Heiligenstadt Testament Beethoven presents his deafness in a dramatic manner that corresponds only partially with the accounts of other witnesses. The composers Carl Czerny[67] and Ignaz von Seyfried,[68] both of whom had frequent contact with Beethoven, did not recollect noticing any loss of hearing in Beethoven during the first few years after 1800. Ferdinand Ries, writing at the time of the Heiligenstadt Testament, does describe a walk during which his teacher became 'remarkably quiet and gloomy' when Ries drew his attention to the sound of a shepherd's pipe, and he could not hear it. On the whole, however, Ries gives a rather different account: 'In 1802 Beethoven had already . . . suffered impairment of his hearing several times, but the trouble went away again. He found the onset of his deafness such a sensitive subject that one had to be very careful to speak louder, so as not to make him conscious of his deficiency. If he had failed to hear something he usually ascribed it to absence of mind, and he was indeed extremely absent-minded.'[69]

At first Beethoven tried many therapeutic treatments for his deafness. In his letter to Wegeler of 16 November 1801, quoted above, he says: *For some months* [Dr] *Wering has been applying to both arms vesicatories* [a treatment designed to cause blisters] *made, as you will know, from the bark of a certain tree, which is a most uncomfortable cure in that I am always deprived of the free use of my arms for a few days, not to mention the pain.* He sometimes tried shock treatments such as cold showers. After 1816 he used an ear trumpet, and two years later began communicating through the conversation books – notebooks in which people wrote down what they wanted to say to him.

A letter to Wegeler of 2 May 1810 contains the passage: *I would be happy, perhaps one of the happiest of men, if the demon had not taken up residence in my ears – had I not read somewhere that while there is still a good deed for him to do, man may not depart this life of his own free will, I would have been dead long ago – and by my own hand – ah, how beautiful is life, but for me it is poisoned forever.*[70] But it appears that Beethoven's complaints, although they never ceased entirely, became less frequent in the years after the Heiligenstadt Testament.

Beethoven's deafness was, at least for a time, less of a handicap in his musical activities than in everyday life: in late 1813 he was still able to conduct the spectacular première of the 'Battle Symphony', and a few months later he performed publicly as a pianist for the last time in the première of the 'Archduke' Trio Op 97. On the 25 December in 1816 he conducted a performance of his Seventh Symphony at a charity concert in the Hospital of St Marx. The audience probably overlooked certain deficiencies of precision on the revered master's part, but there is no indication that his appearance was a pure formality, as it was later with the performance of the Ninth Symphony. According to Carl Czerny, Beethoven's deafness became 'so severe that he cannot hear the music any more' only around 1817.[71]

To trace Beethoven's attitude to his physical sufferings over the years, we must go back to a remark the young musician made in his journal in December 1793: *Courage, even amidst all physical weaknesses, shall rule my mind. I have known them* [the physical weaknesses] *25 years, this year must determine the complete man – nothing must remain.*[72] If we complete that last comment by adding 'but the works of the mind', it becomes clear what Beethoven understood by 'the complete man': not the growth in common of body, spirit and mind, but total concentration on those powers that would be of use to his vocation.

Beethoven did not simply scorn desire or more mundane pleasures. In the letters to Amenda and Wegeler discussed above, he expresses a wish to follow the dictates of his lively and ardent temperament, to participate in social amusements, travel the world, bind himself to an *enchanting girl* and find happiness in marriage. Yet these wishes do not seem wholly real, since he clearly saw them already in the context of their unattainability. What, we may wonder, stood in the way of their satisfaction? In Beethoven's diary entry of 1793 his own mind already demanded the renunciation of earthly joys. Now fate required it, under a new name: deafness. He must now put private happiness behind him, no longer of his own free will but because of his progressive disorder.

Had Beethoven been so successful, popular and indeed beloved in his early years in Vienna that he feared neglecting his vocation out of sheer love for life? Did he simply distrust happiness? It seems he inscribed the word 'Fate' on a certain page of his private biography and to a great extent came to identify it with 'Deafness'. We should not speculate whether perhaps his unconscious mind anticipated or even summoned that deafness. What is certain is that it gave him an opportunity to renounce the world.

That renunciation is first presented as a struggle: he must *grasp Fate by the throat*. But soon afterwards, in the Heiligenstadt Testament, a more elevated and philosophical kind of resignation gets the upper hand: he is not concerned now with real, earthly life, only with the demands of morality and art. The remarks put into Beethoven's mouth in 11 August 1810 by Bettine von Arnim (1785–1859) – in what is presumably an imaginary letter, but one composed after extensive conversations with the composer – are characteristic. Beethoven complains: *My ears, alas, alas, are a barrier through which I cannot easily have any friendly communication with others.* In the same breath he speaks of *this absurd [life] to which, with the best will in the world, one cannot listen.*[73] Communication with the world is not only impossible but unnecessary, since he knows in advance that it would be disappointing.

Dorothea von Ertmann

True communication occurs through art instead. An incident thought to date from 1809 casts light on the kind of 'speaking in music' that was the task of Beethoven's life. The child of a friend had died; the friend was Baroness Dorothea von Ertmann (1781–1849), one of the best pianists in Vienna and a woman whom Beethoven also admired personally. According to Anton Schindler (1795–1864), she could divine 'the most secret intentions in Beethoven's works . . . with as much certainty as if they were written out and before her eyes'.[74] When the baroness suffered a grievous loss on the death of what must have been her only son, she expected a visit from Beethoven, but at first waited in vain. Then he did come, and spoke to her *in music.* The baroness apparently told a niece later that: 'Instead of expressing his sympathy in words, and after silently greeting me, he immediately sat down at the piano and improvised for a long time. Who could describe that music in words? I thought I heard choirs of angels celebrating my child's arrival in the realms above.

'I was extremely well received by Beethoven and already have been several times to see him. He is a most unusual man. Great thoughts float through his mind, which he can only express through music. Words are not at his command. His whole culture is very neglected and, apart from his art, he is rough but honest and without pretensions. He says straight out what is on his mind. In his youth, and even now, he has had to struggle with disappointments. This had made him suspicious and grim. He rails against Vienna and would like to leave. "From the Emperor down to the last shoe polisher," he says, "the Viennese are all a worthless lot."' XAVER SCHNYDER VON WARTENSEE, 1811

When Beethoven had finished, he only pressed my hand in silence; too much moved to be able to speak, he left.'[75]

Besides his progressive deafness and the limitations it imposed on his communication with others, Beethoven was particularly distressed by his lack of happiness in love. Probably in 1807, and certainly when he was staying in Baden near Vienna, he tells us how, *when M. drove past and seemed to look at me*, a sigh escaped him: *Only love – yes, only love can give you a happier life – oh God – let me at last find her, the woman who will strengthen me in virtue – who may permissibly be mine.*[76] There were always such obstacles in his way; Beethoven may have seen them in the rank of the lady driving past in her carriage.

Who was this 'M.'? We do not know, and hardly need to. The initial stands like a code for Beethoven's disastrous love life. When he says that a sigh 'escaped' him, this hardly tells the whole story: in fact he noted it down on a piece of paper, almost like a musical theme. As we look more at Beethoven's music, we will see that this sigh functions as a motif of thwarted expectation, which in itself reconciles him to his loss, even compensates him for it. The letters to the 'Immortal Beloved', quoted below complete because they are central to any biography of Beethoven, reveal a similar pattern.

*On 6 July, in the morning.*

*My angel, my all, my Self – only a few words today, and those in pencil – (in yours) – I shall not know until tomorrow where I am lodging; what*

On 28 or 29 June 1812 Beethoven set off for Prague. He stopped off on 1 July at the 'Black Horse' hotel. On 2 July he met with Karl August Varnhagen of Ense and made an appointment to see him the following evening. Beethoven missed this rendezvous and he himself thought it was *'almost rude'* to do so, though obviously something had come up. On 4 July Beethoven carried on towards Teplitz. He got there on 5 July, at about 4 in the morning, lodged in the 'Golden Sun'. What kept Beethoven from his meeting on 3 July, we do not yet know.

Last page of the letter to the 'Immortal Beloved', 7 July 1812

a useless waste of time such things are – why this deep grief where necessity speaks? Can our love continue except through sacrifices, through not demanding all? Can you change the fact that you are not entirely mine, I am not entirely thine – Ah God, look at the beauty of nature and calm your mind over what must be – love demands all, and rightly too, so it is to me with you, to you with me – *only you forget so easily that I must live* for myself and for you, *if we were entirely united, you would not mind that any more than I do* – I had a dreadful journey and did not get here until four in the morning; since there were not enough horses the posting coach chose another route for the journey, but what a terrible road; at the last stage but one I was warned that we would be travelling by night, and they threatened me with a forest, but I was merely intrigued, and there I was wrong, the carriage had to set off along that terrible road for no good reason, a mere country track, and without two such postillions as I had I would have never have arrived – Esterhazy, coming here by the other, more usual route suffered the same fate with 8 horses as I did with four – however, then I felt quite cheerful again, as I always do when I am lucky enough to surmount some obstacle – now, let us quickly move on from externals to what really matters, we shall see each other soon, I cannot tell you today what ideas of my life I have been forming during these last few days – if our hearts were always close to each other I would probably have no such thoughts, my breast is full of much that I must tell you – ah, there are moments where I find speech useless – be of good cheer – remain my true and only treasure, my all, as I am thine – as for the rest, may the gods send, what must and shall be for us –

   *Thy faithful Ludwig.*

*Monday evening, 6 July –*

   You are suffering, my dearest creature – only now do I discover that letters must be handed in early in the morning on Mondays – Thursdays – the only days when the post goes from here to K. – you are suffering – ah, wherever I am you are with me, I tell us both that I will arrange matters so that I can live with you, what a life!!!! thus!!!! Without you – pursued hither and thither by people's kindness that I think I wish to deserve as little as I do deserve it – Humility man to men – it gives me pain – and when I consider what I am in the universe, and what he is that they call the greatest – and yet here again is the divine part of mankind – I weep when I think that you will probably not receive your first news of me until Saturday – however much you love me I love you more – but never hide yourself from me – good night – as I am taking the waters I must go to sleep now. Ah God – so near! so far! Is not our love a true heavenly structure – and as strongly founded as the firmament.

*7 July, A good morning*

   Still in bed, my Immortal Beloved, I send my thoughts hastening to you, thoughts sometimes happy, sometimes sad, waiting to discover whether Fate will hear us – I can live only entirely with you or not at all, yes, I have determined to wander abroad until I can fly to your arms and say I have entirely come home to you, until I can send my soul enveloped by you into the spiritual realm – yes, alas, it must be so – you may be all the more at rest in knowing how faithful I am to you, no other woman can ever have my heart, never – never – Oh God, why must one leave what one loves so much, yet my life in V. is now a wretched one – your love makes me both the happiest and unhappiest of men – at my age I need some steady equilibrium in my life – can this be so in our circumstances? Angel, I have just learnt *that the post goes every day – so I must conclude if you are to get my letter directly – be calm, only by considering our existence calmly can we attain our end and live together – be calm – love me – today – yesterday – what longing with tears I feel for you – you – you – my life – my all – farewell – oh, love me still – never doubt the true heart of thy beloved*

*L.*

*Ever thine – ever mine – ever ours [77]*

There is no mention of the person to whom the letters are addressed, the dates do not mention the year, the place to which they are sent is abbreviated to 'K.', and all that is clear is that the writer is in a spa, so at first there seem very few points of reference for placing the letters at any definite point in Beethoven's life. However, research into the subject using almost forensic methods has shown that with overwhelming probability they were written from Teplitz to a lady in Karlsbad in 1812. But who is that 'angel'? Scarcely a woman who features in the story of Beethoven's life has not been identified with her. All the years of Beethoven scholarship has failed to reach any firm conclusion. But even if we knew beyond all doubt who the letters' recipient was, we still could not be sure whether she was the Immortal Beloved. Indeed, were these letters, which were found among Beethoven's papers after his death, ever sent at all? Are fact and fiction perhaps intermingled? We may at least assume that the letters are not simply spontaneous outpourings about his situation at the time: they also present his views on love in general.

Love was absent from the Heiligenstadt Testament, that other 'fragment of a great confession', to use Goethe's description. Now Beethoven was striving to achieve renunciation in love as well. For there is no mistaking that in spite of all their passion, the 'thoughts' hastening towards the Immortal Beloved are gloomy. Love is indeed the highest imaginable good, a *heavenly structure* dispensing the utmost happiness. In Beethoven's case, however, that happiness is to be given for brief moments, if at all. The *circumstances* do not allow a lasting relationship; reality immediately demands distance, sacrifice, renunciation.

While such an attitude of resignation is partly concealed here by stormy assurances of passion, it is very much present in another document. Also in 1812, Beethoven began a journal – now extant only in copies – with the words: *Submission, deepest submission to your fate*, and continued: *In this manner with A. everything goes to ruin.*[78]

Another cipher – and here not even the abbreviation 'A' can be entirely trusted, since the copyist may have misread it. We might begin to think it is impossible to track the reality, as opposed to the image, of the composer's life. Whether by his own wish, or through the chances whereby the sources have come down to us, we always encounter the same almost abstract pattern of thwarted emotion. The comings and goings of everyday life, the vicissitudes of love and desire do not feature.

Did everyday life exist for Beethoven at all? Can we have any confidence in the picture of him cheerfully courting ladies, at least in the first decade of his life in Vienna? He 'liked women very much, particularly beautiful, youthful faces, and when we passed a charming girl he would usually turn round, examine her again closely through his glass, and laugh or smile when he saw me noticing him. He was very often in love, but usually only for a short period. When I once teased him over the conquest of a lovely lady, he admitted that she had attracted him very strongly for a long time – namely seven whole months.' So Ferdinand Ries remembered,[79] and Wegeler tells us that, 'in Vienna, at least while I was living there, Beethoven was always involved in amorous relationships, and sometimes made conquests that would have been hard, if not impossible, for many an Adonis to achieve.'[80]

　　　　　　　　　　　　　　　　　　　　　　　　　　　　　　　　　　　LOVE

'One day I went to see him in Baden in order to continue my studies. There I found a beautiful young lady sitting with him on the sofa. Since it seemed to me that my arrival had been inopportune, I started to go away again immediately. But Beethoven held me back and said 'play for us awhile.' He and the lady remained sitting behind me. I had been playing for a long time when Beethoven suddenly called out 'Ries, play something amorous.' Then a little while later, 'something melancholy.' Then, 'something impassioned.' From what he told me I gathered that he must have offended the lady somewhat and that he now wanted to humour her. Finally, he jumped up and shouted. 'Those are all things I wrote!' I had, as it happens, played parts of his own composition, linked together with short connecting passages, but this seemed to have pleased him. The lady soon went away and to my great astonishment, Beethoven did not know who she was . . .'

FERDINAND RIES

Yet Wegeler's comment refers to the time when Beethoven, as mentioned before, was reputedly rejected by the singer Magdalena Willmann for his ugly appearance and eccentricity. We may also doubt whether Beethoven was open to making 'conquests' without marriage in mind. He certainly had a tendency towards strict morality, and conveyed it clearly, not least to his younger brothers. He expressly adjured Nikolaus Johann in 1796: . . . *do beware of the whole pack of bad women.*[81] In 1823 he still had not forgiven his brother Kaspar Karl for marrying a woman in 1806 whom he, Ludwig, considered wanton – and doing so, moreover, only after the birth of their son Karl: *Even my brother's marriage demonstrates both his immorality and his lack of understanding.*[82]

When an approach to the married pianist Marie Bigot in 1807 was obviously misinterpreted in her circle, Beethoven wrote two letters full of explanations and apologies to Marie and her husband: . . . *In any case it is one of my first principles never to be in any relationship with another man's wife but that of friendship.* And he adds: . . . *You will never find me less than honourable, for I learned to love virtue – and all that is fine and good – from my childhood days.*[83]

We do not know how far Beethoven followed these maxims in real life. On the one hand he obviously made formal proposals of marriage to women when success was unlikely; on the other there were encounters which at least allow scope for speculation. Beethoven's approach to Countess Giulietta Guicciardi (1784– 1856) in 1801 is one such incident. Whether the countess, then 17 years old to Beethoven's 30, was the *dear enchanting girl* of the 1801 letter to Wegeler cannot be said for certain. At any rate, Beethoven was giving her piano lessons in her parents' house at that time and, according to surviving family correspondence,[83] she was interested in accepting Beethoven's amorous advances as well as the dedication of the Sonata in C Minor Op 27 No 2, later known as the 'Moonlight' Sonata. But in 1803 she married the noted ballet composer Count Wenzel Robert Gallenberg, who was scarcely a year older than her.

Twenty years later Beethoven gave an account of the affair in conversation with Anton Schindler. Using French, the language of discretion, he jotted down in his conversation book awkward comments which suggest his wounded feelings at the time. They also show how, in retrospect, he used

Countess Giulietta Guicciardi

to dramatize his sense of hurt. The gist of what he told Schindler was as follows: *She loved me more than ever she loved her husband. Yet he was more her lover than I, but through her I learned of his misfortune and found a prosperous man who gave me the sum of 500 gulden to help him. He was always my enemy, and for that very reason I did him all the good imaginable . . .* Beethoven went on to say that on a later occasion Giulietta visited him in tears, but he repulsed her.

We do not know how far Beethoven's account, dating as it does from 1823, was based on reality. Nor should we assume that he made little impression on women because a few thought him ugly and untidy. As the dramatist and poet Franz Grillparzer (1791–1872) remembered him, he was 'carefully, indeed elegantly dressed; only later did he neglect his person to the point of uncleanliness.'[85] Carl Czerny gives a similar account: 'In his earlier years (up to about 1810) his dress was elegant and his behaviour cavalier-like; later, however, as his deafness increased, he became more and more unkempt.'[86] The pencil sketch by Ludwig Schnorr von Carolsfeld on page 75 shows Beethoven, then about 38, with a certain elegance about him and still looking quite young. The famous drawing by Peter Lyser on page 107 is from a later period, but does give an impression of how Beethoven may have looked in his early and middle years in Vienna, he cuts an urbane figure, taking an interest in the world. Though his facial expression in the detail looks as if hes is rejecting the world.

A far deeper mark was left on Beethoven's life by his relationship with Josephine von Brunsvik (1779–1821) than by his courting of Giulietta Guicciardi. In such cases it is difficult to distinguish between conjecture and certainty. Beethoven himself, deliberately or unconsciously, seems to have obliterated many traces of his personal life. But in this particular case there is the added difficulty that the Brunsvik family themselves were anxious that no details of Beethoven's relationship with Josephine and her sister Therese should be known for many generations. Not until 1957 did the Beethoven scholar Joseph Schmidt-Görg publish thirteen letters from Beethoven to Josephine, together with the drafts of four of Josephine's own letters, a correspondence conducted between 1804 and 1808, which reveals the intense urgency of Beethoven's courtship.

The Brunsviks, who were, as it happens, related to the

Guicciardis, had estates in Hungary. In May 1799 the girls' widowed mother travelled to Vienna to spend some weeks there and introduce her family into society, hoping to find good marriages for her daughters. Therese and Josephine immediately began taking piano lessons from Beethoven. He was happy to visit the household, often stayed from twelve to five o'clock, and 'never tired of holding my fingers down and bending them, whereas I had been taught to stretch them up and hold them flat.'[87] On a visit to the Müller sculpture gallery the family met its owner, Count Joseph Deym von Střitětž, who asked for Josephine's hand in marriage only a few days later. The 20-year-old girl was not interested in the 'strange old man'[88] – he was 47 years old – but allowed her mother to persuade her into marriage. When it turned out that Deym was in financial difficulties Josephine's mother was indignant; Josephine herself, however, increasingly came to see the positive side of her marriage.

Beethoven visited the Deym-Brunsvik household regularly as a friend. Josephine says of one domestic concert on 10 December 1800: 'Beethoven played the sonata for violoncello, and I the last of the three violin sonatas [Op 12 No 3] with the accompaniment of Schuppanzigh who, like all the others, played divinely. Then Beethoven, like a true angel, let us hear his new quartets [Op 18], not yet engraved, which are the finest of their kind.'[89]

After Deym's death from pneumonia in January 1804 Beethoven courted his beautiful widow with increasing intensity. The idea of giving support to a weak woman with four small children must have given his courtship the moral basis he needed to justify his desire for an amorous relationship. It seems symbolically appropriate that at this time he was working on his opera *Fidelio*, a 'hymn to married love' sung against a background of willingness to make sacrifices.

The Brunsvik family discussed whether a connection was possible and sensible. On 20 January 1805 Therese wrote to her sister

Charlotte: 'Now tell me, what is to become of this business of Pepi [Josephine] and Beethoven? She should be on her guard! I think you were referring to her when you underlined those certain words in the piano score: Her heart must have the power to say no, a sad if not the saddest of all duties!' What compelled Josephine to accept that sad duty? Was it their difference in social standing, or perhaps a presentiment that marriage to Beethoven could not guarantee a suitable upbringing and social life for her children?

Josephine provides only hints in her draft of a letter to Beethoven, saying: 'I would be breaking holy bonds were I to listen to your requests – believe me, it is I who suffer most through doing my duty – and it is certain that my actions were guided by honourable motives.'[90] A draft of a letter from a later period breaks off at a significant point: 'I love you, and value your moral character – you have shown much love and goodwill to me and my children, I shall never forget it, and as long as I live I will always take an interest in your fate and do what I can for your happiness. – But you must not take it ill if I . . .'[91] Josephine also took great care that no one outside the family should know about her closeness to Beethoven.

Did Beethoven truly believe in the possibility of marriage to his *dear, beloved, only* Josephine, his *one woman friend* and *only beloved*, as he put it in his letters?[92] What did he mean by writing, in the spring of 1805: *May our love be of long – long duration – it is so noble – so firmly founded on mutual respect and friendship?*[93] Do these words perhaps already suggest that same renunciation, a precaution against future loss, of ordinary happiness and its sensual fulfilment?

In the same letter, Beethoven tries to play down the fact that everyone obviously guessed with what ardour he had dedicated his song *An die Hoffnung* Op 32 to Josephine. The closing verse of this song, composed in the spring of 1805 while he was working on the second act of *Leonore* (later to become *Fidelio*), speaks for itself:

a man thus marked out by Fate is destined only to find happiness beyond the grave.

Beethoven's letters of the autumn of 1807 suggest that Josephine was by then no longer letting him visit her. She does continue to assure him of her 'friendship', and expresses an interest in news of his welfare. Beethoven seems to have retreated at the same time, and then ended the correspondence. Early in 1810 Josephine married the Estonian Baron Christoph von Stackelberg, whom she had met in the circle of the great Swiss educational reformer Johann Heinrich Pestalozzi (1746–1827) while looking for suitable schools for her children, and whom she had obviously come to value as a suitable man to bring them up.

Perhaps this loss spurred Beethoven to thoughts of marriage. In March 1809 he wrote to his close friend Ignaz von Gleichenstein (1778–1828) at his home in Freiburg im Breisgau: *Well, you can help me look for a wife; if you find a handsome one there in F., a lady who might perhaps devote a sigh to my harmonies from time to time . . . then let me know.*[94] This may have been meant as a joke, but Beethoven was very much in earnest early in 1810 when he asked for the hand of the 19-year-old Therese Malfatti (1792–1851). She was the niece of his doctor Johann Malfatti, who described him as 'a confused fellow – yet he can be the greatest genius.'[95] He asked Gleichenstein to get him *some linen or Bengal cloth for shirts, and at least half a dozen cravats,*[96] he had suits made, and borrowed a mirror from Zmeskall to replace one that he had broken.[97] He asked Wegeler to send on a baptismal certificate – apparently in preparation for the formalities of a marriage. But matters never reached that point, for he was rejected.

He may have been consoled by the 25-year-old Bettine Brentano, later von Arnim. Goethe, then 60, had courted this young woman a year earlier. Now visiting a relation she turned Beethoven's head. After Beethoven's death she contributed to his myth by publishing

Therese Malfatti

Bettine Brentano, later von Arnim

three letters allegedly addressed to her; only the second is certain to be authentic.

The letters to the 'Immortal Beloved' themselves, as suggested above, must be seen as part of the Beethoven myth. There is a good deal to suggest that they were addressed to Josephine, whose marriage was already in such difficulties by July 1812, that there was possibly a reconciliation with Beethoven. Even Marie-Elisabeth Tellenbach's conjecture that Josephine's daughter Minona, born on 8 April 1813, was Beethoven's child,[98] cannot be dismissed entirely. On the other hand no one can produce evidence of a meeting between Josephine and Beethoven in Prague or Karlsbad in the summer of 1812, so that Maynard Solomon's claim, supported by various biographical details, that the 'Immortal Beloved' was Antonie von Brentano (1780–1869),[99] does demand serious scrutiny.

At the time, however, Antonie, although a faithful friend of Beethoven's, seems to have been happily married to Franz Brentano

Josephine von Brunsvik

Antonie von Brentano

'The Immortal Beloved': Two candidates. Antonie von Brentano (1780–1869), born in Vienna, married a merchant, Franz Brentano (1765–1844) in 1798 and moved to Frankfurt to live with him there. She returned to Vienna from 1809 to 1812 and became, at the least, an intimate friend of Beethoven. The Brentanos returned to Frankfurt in 1812 but remained good friends. Beethoven dedicated the Diabelli Variations Op 120 to Antonie. Countess Josephine Deym, née Brunsvik (1779–1821) came from a family of Hungarian aristocrats. She was a very musical child and came to know Beethoven after visiting Vienna in 1799. She married Count Joseph Deym in 1799; he died in 1804. Beethoven seems to have been in love with her from about 1804 to 1807 (several love letters from him survive) and he wrote the song *An die Hoffnung* (To Hope) Op 32 for her. Josephine's feelings are less clear and it is not certain that they ever met again after 1807. She married a second time, to Baron Christoph von Stackelberg, in 1810.

(1765–1844), Bettine's stepbrother. On 26 January 1811 she had written to her brother-in-law Clemens about Beethoven in terms which may be interpreted as admiration but hardly as a confession of passionate love: 'I would like to place the original [of the text of a cantata sent to her] in the sanctified hands of Beethoven, whom

I deeply honour, who moves like a divine figure among the living, whose elevated view of the world below and whose ailing body can only momentarily put him out of humour, for Art embraces him, pressing him to her warm heart.'[100] Still, if there was a close friendship between them, Beethoven felt and interpreted it with far greater passion than Antonie herself.

Many of the aforementioned records of Beethoven's life, particularly the two important texts found after his death – the Heiligenstadt Testament and the letters to the 'Immortal Beloved' – might convey the impression of a man who suffered from his worldly existence, often plunged in gloom, and yearning for love, rather than finding fulfilment in it. That may well be true. Goethe, who met Beethoven at the Bohemian spa of Teplitz barely two weeks after the letters to the 'Immortal Beloved' were written, said of him: 'I am afraid he is a wholly untamed character, who may not be wrong in finding the world detestable, but that does nothing to make it a more enjoyable place either for himself or for others.'[101] But this attitude left plenty of scope for very different kinds of conduct and experience, including the enjoyment of ordinary pleasures, friendship and social intercourse.

Beethoven was not able to run a household efficiently. His complaints about careless and dishonest servants were endless, and he changed his residence in Vienna so often that his various movements are too many to list. There is no doubt that Beethoven was suspicious and miserly, and often treated his servants badly. His cooks and manservants must frequently have found him an impossible employer; they only stayed until they could find a better post.

His rudeness became something of a deliberate pose. When his music copyist Ferdinand Wolanek wrote Beethoven a civil letter protesting against his verbal abuse, he wrote on it: *Is one to pay compliments to such a wretched fellow, a man who steals one's money? No, one pulls his asinine ears instead.* He goes on: *You slovenly, stupid scribe! It would be more fitting for you to correct the mistakes you make yourself out of ignorance, overweening pride, arrogance and stupidity than try to instruct me, for that is as if a sow were to instruct Minerva.*

*Beethoven.*[102]

Nonetheless Beethoven was lucky enough to find faithful and understanding people to help him. A note of April 1809 to his friend Baron Nikolaus von Zmeskall is typical: *My dear Z. Suitable lodgings have just been found for me – but I need someone to help me in this matter, I can't rely on my brother because he never recommends anything but the cheapest – so tell me at what time you and I can go and see these lodgings today – they are in the Klepperstall.*[103] Ferdinand Ries, who found Beethoven lodgings in 1804 in the Pasqualati house on the Mölkerbastei with a fine view of the old city, the suburbs and the mountains just outside Vienna, remembered: 'He left several times, but kept coming back, so that as I later heard Baron Pasquillati [sic] said good-humouredly enough, when Beethoven moved out: "We won't let those lodgings; Beethoven will be back again."'

Before Beethoven moved to the Mölkerbastei he had shared lodgings in the 'Red House' on the Alservastadt 'glacis' with

'One day we were dining at the Swan; the waiter brought him the wrong dish. Beethoven had scarcely said a few choice words about it, which the waiter had answered perhaps not quite so politely as he should have, when Beethoven laid hold of the dish (it was a so-called 'Lungenbratel' with lots of sauce) and flung it at the waiter's head. The poor fellow still had on his arm a large number of plates . . . and could do nothing to help himself; the sauce ran down his face. He and Beethoven shouted and cursed at each other, while all the other guests laughed out loud. Finally Beethoven began laughing at the sight of the waiter, who licked with his tongue the sauce that was running down his face, tried to go on hurling insults, but had to go on licking instead . . .'

FERDINAND RIES
*Remembering Beethoven,* 1838

Stephan von Breuning. Everyday arguments were enough to make Beethoven condemn his friend out of hand. On detecting a *mean spirit* in Breuning over a matter of the rent he broke with him; *and now we are no longer friends*, he wrote of Breuning to Ferdinand Ries, continuing: *No, he will never again claim the place in my heart he once had. A man who can ascribe such low thoughts to his friend, and permits himself to treat that friend in so mean a manner too, is not worthy of my friendship.*[104] It was mainly on account of the concessions of Breuning, who is described as a very patient man, that a reconciliation was possible. In later years Beethoven would again find a warm family atmosphere in the home of Breuning and his wife.

Overbearing as he was, Beethoven evidently thought it normal, perhaps even charming, to insult a man one day and ask his pardon the next. *Don't you come to see me any more, sir! You're a false dog, and devil take all false dogs*, he wrote to a friend (once thought by scholars to be the young pianist and composer Johann Nepomuk Hummel), only to write next day: *My dear Natzerl! You're an honest fellow and you were right, I see that now, so come and see me this afternoon, you'll find Schuppanzigh here as well and the two of us will pinch pull and shake you about, what fun. Your friend Beethoven, also known as dumpling, salutes you.*[105]

It is difficult to decide how much of this is spontaneous warmth and how much a pose of geniality. Beethoven sprinkles his letters to Zmeskall with clichés, jokes and joshing wordplay, often at the expense of the recipient, who had to accept being the target of good-humoured banter. Beethoven addresses him *Baron Muck-Carter, Carnival Rogue* and *Confounded Former Little Count of Music.*[106]

To his pupils, Beethoven could show great kindness. Ferdinand Ries tells us: 'In my father's letter of recommendation to Beethoven, he also opened a small credit account for me with him, in case I should need it. I never drew on it, but once, when Beethoven realized that I was short of cash, he gave me some money unasked, and never wanted it back again.'[107] Indeed, a letter from Beethoven to Ries of 1803 runs: . . . *Why did you hide your need from me? None of my friends shall want while I have anything myself.*[108]

It was mainly to those around him that Beethoven turned for the outward and inward necessities of life: money, lodgings, a homely domestic ambience, friendship, social intercourse and emotion. He certainly gave as well as took, and was by no means unwilling to help others, but he assumed

Ferdinand Ries

that it was natural for his friends to enable him to devote his life entirely to art. He was one of the first artists to have made his own self a matter of public interest, something that was possible only because those around him wanted the opportunity to identify with a narcissistic figure of the creator. Beethoven could provide modern and 'absolute' art – art for its own sake, the artist for his own sake – so in return should those around him not place themselves at his service?

When Beethoven wanted to escape the stress and strain of real life he took refuge in nature. It offered the experience of unity and meaning denied him by human society. In the solitude of nature Beethoven could be himself. He spent the summer months in the country during almost all of his life in Vienna, and not simply because he wanted rest and recuperation: *My unhappy hearing does not plague me here. In the country it is as if every tree said to me, holy! holy!*, he wrote in a notebook of 1815.[109] Charles Neate recollected that: 'Nature, so to speak, was his nourishment; he positively seemed to live on it.'[110]

In May 1810 Beethoven wrote to Therese Malfatti: *No one can love the country as much as I do – the woods, trees and rocks echo with the sound mankind desires.* And in 1818 he noted in a sketchbook, during a summer visit to Mödling: *Only a few days in this divine place – yearning or craving – liberation or fulfilment.*[111] It is not entirely clear what he meant by those two pairs of linked concepts, but at least one can see that the emotional frustration so characteristic of Beethoven's psyche was most easily resolved in and by nature.

The two major documents Beethoven left attempting to describe that psyche both mention the healing, soothing power of nature. In the postscript to the Heiligenstadt Testament he wishes for one more *pure day of joy . . . in the temple of nature and mankind.* Beethoven encourages the Immortal Beloved to look *at the beauty of nature and calm your mind over what must be.*

Beethoven did not learn to enjoy living in his own body, but he did know a substitute, nature. For him, this had an essentially religious component; nature, being pure refreshment, brings release from the torments of existence and social disappointment, and allows man to merge with a great unity.

Beethoven only adopted the principle of relaxation, and indeed regression inherent in this idea of nature only into his life. In his music, where even in the late works he grappled with the conflicting demands of individual, society and existence, he was

Page from the score of the Sixth Symphony ('Pastoral'). Beethoven wrote at the bottom of the page: 'NB: write the words nightingale, quail and cuckoo in the parts for the first flute, first oboe, and first and second clarinet, just as they are here in the score' always seeking new solutions with his full *capacity for Art*. As he declared to his great friend and supporter Archduke Rudolph in 1819: *Freedom and progress are the aim, in the world of art, as in the whole of great creation.*[112]

## THE WORKS IN THE 'HEROIC STYLE'

By 1800, the 29-year-old Beethoven already looked like the heir of Haydn and Mozart. He was buoyed up by the awareness of being a Prometheus of his time – a bringer of light not only to the realm of music but to intellectual life as a whole. When Bettine von Arnim visited him in Vienna in 1810 she saw in him 'the builder of a new and sensuous foundation for the intellectual life'; later, in her epistolary novel *Goethes Briefwechsel mit einem Kinde* (Goethe's Correspondence with a Child), thinking of this encounter, she puts these words into his mouth: 'Tell Goethe this from me: tell him that he must hear my symphonies, and then he will acknowledge that I am right, that music is the only incorporeal entrance to a higher world of knowledge, which embraces mankind [but in such a way] that he cannot comprehend it. – A rhythm of the mind is the way to grasp the essence of music: it brings a premonition, the inspiration of heavenly knowledge, and what the mind senses of it is the incarnation of intellectual understanding.'[113]

We do not know exactly how far Bettine was mingling fact and fiction, but she expressed what the educated world of her time thought of the composer: Beethoven raises the art of music to an entirely new level. He makes it 'absolute', so that it need not be understood either as merely having a social function, or as an art lending its powers to the service of a text, dramatic subject or pictorial model. Music says what cannot be said in words, music is pure spirit, although still more sensuously close to us than any other art.

The two musical enthusiasts Ludwig Tieck and Wilhelm Heinrich Wackenroder were the first to write of the absolute nature of music in *Phantasien über die Kunst* (Fantasies on Art), published in 1799. To them, it was basically unimportant what sounds they utilized to withdraw 'quietly into the land of music, as if into the land of faith',[114] where a presentiment of the absolute might be felt. Rather, what mattered was their 'devout' attitude to music. But this subjective concept of absolute music is not adequate to understand the compositions of Beethoven. With the works of what is often called his heroic phase, Beethoven entered that narrow circle of poets and thinkers who deliberately and directly grapple with the transcendent and the inexorable.

Beethoven had his own expression for the absolute: Fate. A line in Goethe's *Egmont*, for which Beethoven wrote the incidental music in the year 1810 when Bettine visited him, is certainly very much in that spirit: 'As if lashed by invisible spirits, Phæton's horses of time gallop on with the flimsy chariot of our fate, and there is nothing we can do but hold fast with courage to the reins.' But Beethoven did not think the point of his existence was solely to endure, but that his work could open up real dialogue with the fate and meet it with super-human self-confidence.

The 'Work' is the spirit objectified, reminiscent of the grief stricken Beethoven incapable of putting his condolences into words, speaking in music with Dorothea von Ertmann after the loss of her child. For such a composer, capturing the world meant giving it that higher, ideal sense which reality often enough concealed from him.

With Beethoven, music was no longer what it had been before; learned or playful works, art commissioned for entertainment, the depiction of emotions, the expression of feelings or religious devotion. It is philosophy in sound, participating in the ideas and intellectual currents of its time. These ideas and currents are not used by the composer as the subject of programme music, but cast in their own individual form, which makes sense without even detailed knowledge of the composer's personal experiences or his confrontation with the spirit of the age. The difficulty of determining in detail the form of the music and the thought behind it does not alter the fact that the whole can be understood only as their mutual interaction.

A comparison of the Piano Sonata in F Minor Op 2 No 1 with the 'Pathétique' Sonata Op 13 and the 'Tempest' Sonata Op 31 No 2 clearly shows how swiftly Beethoven put his new musical concept into practice. The first movement of the Sonata in F minor, described on page 21, is already entirely characteristic of Beethoven in its driven quality and succinct expression, but at the same time very conventional in its fidelity to the strictures of sonata form.

In many respects the 'Pathétique' ('moving' or 'full of pathos'), published only three years later, is wider in scope. Even its name carries a certain weight: apart from 'Les adieux' ('Farewells') Op 81a, it is the only descriptive title Beethoven himself gave a piano sonata. The power of the musical language is stronger, the range

Sonata originally (in the 16th century) meant simply something played rather than sung. Over two centuries it came to mean a piece in several movements, written for solo piano or piano accompanying another instrument. By the time of and under the influence of Mozart, Haydn and Beethoven, the sonata had developed into a classical form of usually three movements, fast – slow – fast. Sonata form is a term used to describe not the overall form of the sonata but a particular musical structure used for single movements, most commonly the first, not just of sonatas, but of many other kinds of music as well – symphonies, string quartets, concertos, etc. A movement in sonata form consists of three sections: the exposition, in which two (or sometimes more) musical phrases, motifs or melodies are introduced; the development, in which the composer elaborates and plays freely with those motifs; and the recapitulation, which repeats the exposition but with modifications.

of keys is wider, and the keyboard writing is almost orchestral in colour, making greatly increased claims for the piano. Sonata form is no longer an obligatory norm, but the point of departure for individual design. We can see this in the first movement of the sonata. It begins with a weighty phrase marked *grave* (slow and solemn), which is not just the introduction, but sets the tone at the beginning of the development section. Shortly before the conclusion of the movement, it concentrates musical power, loads the composition with dark pathos, and – particularly in light of the title, 'Pathétique' – has an obvious meaning. This can be read from the first phrase alone, a phrase consisting of a single bar: the striking formal rhythm suggests weight, the diminished seventh chord emphasized as a suspension on the third bar suggests excitement, while the falling second at the end is to be understood in the traditional way as a sigh.

This is all eloquently articulated in a single breath. The Beethoven scholar Harry Goldschmidt has been much criticized for wondering whether such phrases can be read like verbal texts,[115] but there is no mistaking that here, as elsewhere, Beethoven's composition is partly rhetorical, as if the piano were a human voice. As the piece develops, this phrase is repeated with urgent intensification, moving ever higher up the scale. Again the rhetorical nature of the phrase is clear. After a few bars this accumulated energy dies away: a rapid downward run leads to the *Allegro di molto e con brio* (very lively and spiritedly) element with all the passionate anguish that one finds in the writing of the 'Sturm und Drang' ('Storm and Stress') movement.

Both the *Grave* and the *Allegro* elements penetrate each other in the development. One is reminded of Beethoven's remark to Wegeler in 1801: *I will grasp Fate by the throat, it shall not bring me down entirely*. Those words are certainly not the 'programme' for the first movement of the 'Pathétique', but there is an analogous sense of rebellion against oppressive experiences.

This sonata is an advance over the Sonata in F minor Op 2 No 1 both in structure and meaning. The composition is much more varied and subtle, its contrasts, correspondences and intensifications most skilfully worked out. By comparison with the youthful, sinewy sound of the early sonata, that of the later work seems fuller and better developed, if also more anguished. In the 'Pathétique' the composer does not content himself with presenting a single attitude – as he tended to do in the first movement of the sonata Op 2 No 1 – but instead offers a subtly varied landscape.

Only a few years later Beethoven took another step; the first movement of the Sonata in D minor Op 31 No 2 no longer represents a typical attitude or character, nor expresses a distinct intellectual experience. From the first, the music is very much itself. The *Largo* (slow) phrase rises as a spread chord like a shadowy outline emerging from primeval mists. The following *Allegro* (quick) element, sharply contoured in rhythm and melody, hastens forward and encounters the *Largo* at close quarters, creating great tension.

The six opening bars do not represent a regularly constructed phrase, are not beautiful, nor even immediately plausible in psychological or rhetorical terms, although they can easily be placed in the tradition of the chordal and figurative prelude. They are, to echo the words of Bettine von Arnim, a 'rhythm of the mind'. In this sonata Beethoven is not giving musical outline to an easily grasped theme, as he still was in the 'Pathétique' – he is thinking.

It is fascinating to trace the way this train of thought goes on; the introduction is followed by an immaculately constructed main theme, energetic in manner and yet too conventional to remain at the heights of the introduction.

Its stability is of course challenged, particularly in that section of the first movement that in traditional sonata form would have constituted the recapitulation, where – like the whole section – it has in effect played itself out. Instead, we hear the opening bars again, but interrupted by a two-part recitative to be performed *con espressione e semplice* (with expression and simplicity). The ideas of the opening are picked up again and at the same time powerfully extended: the tension dissolves in a 'sigh'. The actual meaning of this sigh remains an open question, but its appearance is the most important outcome of this movement: an outcome not required by sonata form, but reached by free intellectual activity.

Shortly after 1800 Beethoven is reported to have said that he was *not greatly satisfied* with his music to date, and was thinking of taking *a new path*. Carl Czerny, the source for this remark, adds that 'the partial result of this decision'[116] was to be seen in the piano sonatas op 31, thus showing how acutely Beethoven's contemporaries perceived the ways in which he was innovating. Years later Anton Schindler, violinist and rather unreliable biographer of Beethoven, asked the master for the 'key' to an understanding of the Piano Sonata Op 31 No 2 (and to the Sonata Op 57); music like the opening movement of Op 31 No 2 does not readily disclose its

Carl Czerny (1791–1857) was a successful Viennese pianist, teacher and composer. His pupils included Beethoven's ill-fated nephew Karl and the 9-year-old Franz Liszt. A pupil and friend of Beethoven, he was deeply knowledgeable about Beethoven's piano compositions. He was a prolific composer of solo and chamber music for the piano, but is most widely remembered for his collections of piano études. His memoirs include many interesting reminiscences of Beethoven.

meaning to the hearer through reference to formal conventions, association, or programmatic interpretation.

Beethoven's answer to Schindler, *Read Shakespeare's* Tempest,[117] if authentic, is sibylline but by no means meaningless. It indicates the elevated plane on which the composer, described by his contemporaries as 'a musical Shakespeare',[118] wished his work to be discussed. It is not surprising that Richard Wagner, in his *Art and Revolution*, credited Beethoven with lending music 'masculine, independent poetic force'.[119]

In his memoirs, the composer Hector Berlioz wrote about the years 1827–28: 'I had just experienced Shakespeare and Weber one after the other; not much later, I saw the powerful Beethoven rise at a different point on the horizon. He shook me almost as severely as Shakespeare had done. He opened a new world for me with his music, just as the Bard had discovered a new universe for me with his poetry.' To place Beethoven on the same level as Shakespeare was – according to Nietzsche – 'the boldest craziest thought'.

The point illustrated here through the three piano sonatas is even more relevant to Beethoven as a symphonic composer. A dozen years were enough for him to create an idea of symphonic music that would last the century and set the standard first in Vienna, then in Europe, and finally all over the world. By 1812, the year of the Seventh and Eighth Symphonies, Beethoven could look back on symphonic work that had made him an undisputed colossus in that field.

Beethoven did not lack models for his new and very distinct understanding of symphonic music. Mozart's three late symphonies, especially the last, the C major so-called 'Jupiter', were particularly important to him. Not until the beginning of the new century did Beethoven find his public, one that could understand the performance of symphonic music as the emblem of a 'musical community',[120] which shared the leading ideas of the time and believed that music united humanity; and this public itself found and encouraged Beethoven. With such a public the genre finally freed itself from the sense of symphony as mere functional music or a divertimento.

In the slow introduction to the First Symphony, we can already see Beethoven working to break free from the idea of the symphony as a specimen of a genre and to create a music more concerned with intellectual process than beautiful melodies, stirring rhythms and well-proportioned forms. The first chords show where we are: they do not strike an emphatic opening accent, or follow tradition by introducing the key or even leading directly towards it; instead they begin with a dissonance resolved in an unexpected tonality, taking an unprecedentedly circuitous route before the fundamental key even comes into sight. Like a bird of prey circling in the air before swooping down on its victim, the symphony finds its theme only after some searching and exploration, but eventually fixes on it with all the more security. To describe this complex process as a 'development' is inadequate – it is intended to express a universal experience. Searching becomes discovery, uncertainty becomes certainty, complexity becomes clarity.

Beethoven understood his task as the concentrated formulation of the ideas of his time. To do so is not an exercise in 'pure' form. The main theme has both an abstract and a historical element; it embodies energy and an urge to move forward, echoing the patriotic music of the French Revolution, such as

Symphony (literally 'sound together') originally designated what we would now call an orchestral overture or an interlude in a larger vocal work. Since the mid-18th century, the term came to mean a large-scale ambitious orchestral work, usually in four movements, with the first movement in sonata form. Haydn and Mozart both decisively developed the classical form of the symphony. Beethoven raised the symphony to a new level of expressiveness and became the often daunting standard against which all subsequent efforts in the genre were judged.

the *Ouverture de la journée de Marathon* by the violinist Rodolphe Kreutzer.

Turning from the First Symphony to the Third, the 'Eroica', we can see more of Beethoven's struggles with the problem of form and content in his treatment of the Promethean myth. As already discussed on page 28, after the public acclaim that greeted his First Symphony, he undertook a ballet, *The Creatures of Prometheus*. This, because of its genre, might have seemed better than a purely instrumental

Beethoven, around 1808 from a drawing by Julius Schnorr von Carolsfeld

composition for giving concrete expression his ideas. Its production on stage meant that there could be little doubt of its message.

But although this approach was successful with the public, it must ultimately have seemed to the composer too flat: it made music not the master but the servant, and ignored its special capacity to say what cannot be said in any other way. Beethoven therefore turned to the subject again and composed not a heroic ballet but a heroic symphony, the 'Eroica'. The Promethean idea, which is at the centre of the action of the ballet, was no longer expressed verbally but treated as a *musical* theme. The festive *contredanse* (country dance) that dominates the finale of the 'Eroica' uses the same theme as the finale of the ballet. In the ballet, the audience see Prometheus, great symbol of the Enlightenment, with his children, rejoicing in the newly created human race. In 'Eroica', however, the music must speak for itself.

RODOLPHE KREUTZER

'I fell quietly asleep and in my dream found myself transported to a concert hall where all the instruments had come to life and were holding a great assembly ... "No!" exclaimed the contrabass, "The devil take anyone who makes us listen to compositions like that every day! I have just come from the rehearsal of a symphony by one of our newest composers, and thought, as you know, I have a very strong and resilient consitution, I could stand it no longer ..."

All of a sudden the property man entered the hall, and all the instruments separated in fear, for they knew the rough hand that packed them up and took them to the rehearsals. "Wait!" he shouted, "Are you rebelling again? Just wait! Pretty soon they are going to set out the *Eroica* symphony by Beethoven, and after that, I'd like to see which one of you can move a limb or a key!"

"Oh, no! Not that!" begged all the instruments.

"Give us an Italian opera: then at least one can get twenty winks from time to time," said the viola ...

I woke up terrified, for in my dreams I was on the way to becoming a great composer of the new school – or a great fool.'

The composer Carl Maria von Weber (1786–1826) indulges in a satirical fantasy.

There are obvious connections, even in the details, between the action of the ballet and the plan of the first movement of the 'Eroica'. If there really is a narrative concealed in the symphony, we might see it as an aid to a composer breaking free from the conventions of symphonic composition, as he had with the sonata, and steering towards a music of the mind. The closing movement is as innovative as the first, presenting a wealth of irreconcilable elements that cannot be equated with either the final recapitulation of a traditional symphony or the affirmative endings of Beethoven's later symphonies.

For some time Beethoven intended either to call the symphony after Napoleon or dedicate it to him; according to Ferdinand Ries his reaction to the news that his hero had had himself crowned emperor in Paris on 2 December 1804 was to tear up the title page with the dedication, exclaiming indignantly: *Is he only an ordinary man after all? Now he will trample all human rights underfoot, merely to indulge his ambition.*[121]

On the title page of the original orchestral parts, published at the end of October 1806, Beethoven actually dedicated the symphony *To the memory of a great man*, clearly indicating someone then dead – perhaps Prince Louis Ferdinand of Prussia, whom Beethoven admired, and who not long before had fallen in the battle of Jena and Auerstädt against the French, a symbol of the struggle of the European nations for freedom from Napoleon.

If such a significant change in the 'hero' personified in the 'Eroica' did take place, it is superfluous to the piece itself.

Napoleon at the Battle of Ercole

Beethoven was concerned with the *idea* of the heroic. His ideals of freedom were inspired by the French Revolution and the coming of Bonaparte to 'fulfil' it, but did not perish with Napoleon himself. The failed revolutionary Richard Wagner, writing from his Swiss exile in 1851, thought that the 'heroic' aspect of the symphony was 'not to be seen as relating solely to a military hero'; rather, a hero was 'the fully rounded man who makes all purely human feelings – of love, of pain and power – his own to the utmost and strongest degree.'[122]

Beethoven's *new path*, discussed above in connection with the Piano Sonata Op 31 No 2, clearly continues in the 'Eroica', which contains almost too many efforts to achieve a subtly differentiated, discursive music going beyond the traditional; it is probably no coincidence that this work is regarded as Beethoven's most difficult symphony. While not impossible to understand, it is indeed difficult because of those innovations of compositional technique which Carl Dahlhaus sees as an expression of the *new way*: 'Musical form,' he writes, appears 'in an emphatic sense as a process, as an urgent, unstoppable movement',[123] enabling audiences to follow it even when the details cannot always be instantly organized into an overall intellectual concept.

There is also a third point: argumentative as Beethoven may be in the 'Eroica', he is also in complete command of the orchestral forces. After the Third his symphonies were no longer concerned merely with the presentation of melodic lines, thematic development and harmonic movement, but also with the ability of the orchestra as a whole to produce musical forms, allowing concentrated sounds to be perceived as a gigantic exchange of energy. The result is a dialogue between intellectual organization and sheer physical force.

The path from the Third to the Fifth Symphony may be marked by a loss of complexity, but there is a gain in cogency. Beethoven does without any verbal programmes (such as the story of Prometheus), hidden allusions to other compositions or subtle philosophical processes; this time developing his concept of the intellectual work of art in a straightforward manner.

Richard Wagner caught this well in a comment which his wife Cosima entered in her diary for 14 July 1880: 'Richard speaks of the C Minor symphony at breakfast, says he has thought about it a great deal, it seems to him as if in this work Beethoven suddenly wanted to lay aside everything of the musician about him and appear in the character of a great popular orator; he spoke in broad terms, says Richard, as if painting al fresco, leaving out all the musical detail that was still so abundantly present, for instance, in the finale of the "Eroica".'[124]

After a good deal of laborious experiment – the first sketches for the main theme of the first movement are somewhat ineffective – Beethoven succeeded in handling the essential thematic material in a stirringly romantic manner. The famous opening motif, a striking succession of four notes, stands clearly in an old tradition of music suggesting awe. It is to be found in Bach's *Christmas Oratorio* and Schubert's song 'Death and the Maiden', where it evokes 'Death on a Pale Horse'.

It does not make much difference, therefore, whether Beethoven's reported remark, *Thus Fate knocks at the door,*[125] is apocryphal or not, it accurately describes the core message of the first movement. Long before Schindler published his memories of Beethoven, contemporaries had noticed the presence of the Fate theme in the Fifth Symphony.[126]

Fate threads its way more conspicuously than any other theme through Beethoven's words. To the examples already given, I will add only, from the period before the Fifth Symphony, a diary entry of 1816: *Show your power, Fate! We are not masters of ourselves; what has been decided must be, and so be it.*[127] That this may be a literary quotation, only serves to reinforce our sense of the prominence of the idea of Fate in contemporary culture.

The struggle of a great soul with Fate is the message of the first movement of the Fifth Symphony. The two themes are each set apart by a pause, seeming particularly to suggest things outside the music. They appear at crucial places, almost like characters in dramatic

MARCEL PROUST *on the Fifth Symphony*
'The music kept creating unity in every one of us, making us feel sometimes alarm, sometimes heroic ardour, sometimes fear, driving out all other ideas and filling us entirely, and now it did the same with our hearts. Can I ever forget what I then felt; just as the wind presses its thousand mouths against every part of the sail to move a ship out to sea, so all those hearts swelled and expanded with endless hope during the Andante of the C minor symphony, like a sail! As the satyrs and the Thyades celebrating the feast of Dionysus only appear to shake their thyrses and place the grapes to their lips, yet the sacred intoxication of the god still reaches them and they feel pain without suffering, and joy more tormenting than pain – so do the two hundred musicians seem to hold little violins.'
*A Sunday at the Conservatoire,* 1895

action – the first of them, the Fate theme, several times and with ever increasing menace, the second, described as *Adagio* (slow), only once, in the first bars of the recapitulation.

The second theme is given to the oboe, an instrument traditionally used to represent the human voice. It articulates a sigh that is the soul's faint but unmistakable protest against Fate and is placed deliberately in the first bars of the recapitulation. According to symphonic tradition, the movement should now come to an end without further incident, but this protest of the soul, voiced by the oboe, shows that Fate, nourished by the energy of the opening 'knocking' theme, is not entirely unopposed. It is a weak protest, but the struggle will go on. There can be no resolution until the end of the symphony.

The second movement makes it clear, that however insistently the rhythm of the 'knocking' theme can still be heard in the background, the idea of a pitiless Fate is beginning to lose its universal relevance. We hear a 'song of hope',[128] at first lyrical and natural, then turning into an energetic fanfare. However, Victory has yet to be won. The tentative transition from the third *Scherzo* (literally, 'joke') movement to the fourth movement finale, which sounds almost like an improvisation and upon which Beethoven hit only at a late stage of composition (the composer and violinist Louis Spohr called it the only touch of genius in the symphony) prepares us to emerge from darkness into light: at the peak of a grandiose crescendo on the dominant seventh chord the victory march appears. The great triumphal song of the crowd now champions the individual soul's defiance of Fate.

Like the 'knocking' motif of the first movement, the hymn-like final theme is both universal and historically specific. Its details and general style it echoes the official music of the French Revolution. The motif that appears later is reminiscent of Rouget de Lisle's *Hymne Dithyrambique*, written to celebrate the fall of

Robespierre. De Lisle (1760–1836) was a French poet and composer whose works include *La Marseillaise*. Beethoven's theme borrows the notes of de Lisle's cry of *la liberté* (freedom).[129] The idea of the individual freeing himself from his Fate is thus not abstract but linked, in however general a sense, with Enlightenment ideas of progress, the French Revolution and Bonapartism.

Beethoven's intellectual art sets leading concepts of his period – in this case mainly concepts of Fate and freedom – in a unique philosophical and musical context. They are identifiable but cannot be simply made explicit. Music communicates in its own way.

There is no mistaking the moral aspect of the struggle with Fate. Beethoven comes to terms with the difficulties of his existence through his music. In the Fifth, he may have been particularly influenced by Schiller, who writes in his essay 'On the Pathetic': 'The first law of tragic art was the presentation of suffering nature. The second is the depiction of moral resistance to suffering.'[130]

At the time of the Enlightenment and the French Revolution, 'Freedom' and 'Nature' are two great concepts often, mentioned in the same breath. The famous Montanvert pavilion, built in the Mont Blanc massif between 1796 and 1799, was originally intended to bear the inscription: 'A la nature par un ami de la liberté.' ('To nature, from a friend of freedom.')[131] In turning so conspicuously to nature, mankind experiences his original freedom and purity; the elevated and refreshing aspects of Nature, shaped by Art, allow man to breathe freely and assume the correct attitude to himself and the world.

Against this background the Sixth 'Pastoral' Symphony, different in character as it is from the Fifth, is the true sister of that work. Written around the same time, both symphonies deal with salvation: in the first it is the reward after a hard struggle, in the second a gift given freely. The finale of the Fifth can be taken as a solemn celebration of victory, that of the Sixth as thanks to the Deity. Those who think that Beethoven definitively found his tone – the heroic tone – in the Fifth will learn better in the Sixth: he can also breathe musical life into the depiction of peaceful nature. After all his intensive work to develop the progress of his theme in the Fifth, his ability to compose in a completely relaxed style from the beginning of the Sixth Symphony is remarkable.

As in the Fifth, there is an extraneous theme at the beginning of the work, separated from the subsequent symphonic development by a pause. This time, however, the theme is not urgent or menacing but tranquil – a pastoral melody like one played on a bagpipe, clearly reminiscent of country tunes from the Danube area.

As this movement, entitled *Awakening of Cheerful Feelings upon Arriving in the Country*, proceeds Beethoven allows himself simply to repeat a section of 46 bars. Nature does not toil but flows easily along. The development is dominated by a rhythmic figure derived from the opening motto, which is played unchanged 32 times, albeit with different harmonic colourings and orchestration.

In key and style the work is in the tradition of the musical pastoral exemplified by works such as Corelli's Concerti Grossi, Bach's *Christmas Oratorio*, Handel's *Messiah* and Haydn's *Seasons*. A symphony composed in 1784 by Justin Heinrich Knecht, then working as a teacher and musician in Biberach, and entitled *Le Portrait musical de la nature* points the way directly ahead to Beethoven, promising the depiction of beautiful landscapes, brooks, singing birds, a storm, a clear sky and a prayer of thanks.

The pastoral genre was highly esteemed in the age of Goethe. According to Schiller, its purpose was 'to show mankind in a state of innocence, that is to say a condition of harmony and peace with itself and with the world outside it'.[132] At the same time Beethoven approaches Hölderlin's religious understanding of nature, which is itself derived from Rousseau. In Hölderlin's 'Rheinhymne' (Hymn to the Rhine) there are lines which seem to point to the second movement of the 'Pastoral', the *Scene by the Brook*:

> *Dann scheint ihm oft das Beste,*
> *Fast ganz vergessen da,*
> *Wo der Stral nicht brennt,*
> *Im Schatten des Walds*
> *Am Bielersee in frischer Grüne zu seyn,*
> *Und sorglosarm an Tönen,*
> *Anfängern gleich, bei Nachtigallen zu lernen.*

('Then it often seems to him best, there almost forgotten, where the sun does not burn down, to be in the shade of the wood, among the fresh green leaves by the Bielersee, free of care and like a beginner learning notes from the nightingales.')[133]

Beethoven too wished to 'learn from the nightingales'. Even in the final score he noted down separately in the parts of the wind instruments the names of the birds they were to 'perform': nightingale, quail and cuckoo. This is the direct imitation of nature. The opening bars of the shepherd's tune introduced by clarinet and horn at the beginning of the last movement are faithful, note for note, to an 'Alphorn tune from the Righi' noted down by H Szadrowsky in 1855. The realistic sound of the storm points to the future of musical tumult. Beethoven achieves this by the means of repeated rapid upward movement in the cellos and basses, always on the same note, so that the two parts cannot be followed separately, but merge into a dull humming sound.

Nature can never be conjured up except as reality. The 'happiness' evoked by country life[134] relies on its concrete reality, not a fantasy, nor an idealization. The birdsong and the music are refreshing in themselves, and do not need to be elaborated or sublimated. However, Beethoven was obviously anxious that the picturesque realism of the Pastoral Symphony should not be over-valued by

A 19th-century romantic view of Beethoven, inspired to compose his Sixth Symphony

audiences and mistaken for the real charm of the symphony; he several times wrote explanatory notes into his sketches and the notation of the score. These comments also found their way into the programme notes for the first performance in the phrase *More of an expression of feeling than a tone-painting*, and were intended to illustrate the fact that the work offered very concrete *reminiscences of country life*, but also presented an artistic expression of the experience recorded in the Heiligenstadt Testament to the effect that *the echo of true joy* was to be felt only *in the temple of nature*. To this day there is aesthetic and musical debate whether the amount of 'programme', that is, the text, images or ideas used as a basis for the music, present in the Sixth Symphony is permissible. But this discussion is both somewhat unproductive. Any supposed contradiction is a false one. The faithful reproduction of nature can be convincingly united with formal severity of design and idealization of the pictorial content, when a great mind is making the attempt.

The 'Eroica', the Fifth and the Sixth are significant examples of the ways in which a symphony can be held together, indeed nourished from first to last movement by the same thematic material. The ideas on which each of these works are based can be plausibly identified: the Promethean idea, victory over the power of Fate, rejuvenation found in nature. Nothing so straightforward can be said about the last three symphonies. Even the chronology of their composition suggests that after writing the Fifth and Sixth Symphonies Beethoven did not approach symphonic music as naturally as before; he presented the first six symphonies to the public within the space of eight years. Another five passed before the performance of the Seventh and Eighth, and then a further gap of nine years between them and his last completed symphony.

The finales of these last symphonies, where Beethoven obviously cannot, indeed feels he must not continue to proclaim the triumph of truth, beauty and virtue, offer clear evidence of his change of direction. The musicologist Hermann Kretzschmar, once very highly regarded, remarked almost indignantly of the finale of the Seventh: 'We come very close to excess here, and would do well, in the interests of young people, to note and to admit that Beethoven was sometimes inclined to pursue his intentions with excessive tenacity.'[135]

The music theorist Carl Dahlhaus speaks of the closing movement of the Eighth as the 'humorous demonstration of the impossibility of resolution'.[136] The C minor leading into a triple *piano* passage in bars 17–18 has become proverbial as a 'note of shock' – Beethoven's friend Louis Spohr felt it was like someone sticking his tongue out in the middle of a conversation.[137] In the choral finale of the Ninth Beethoven would strike out along an entirely new path.

Nonetheless, the Seventh and Eighth can be 'interpreted'. Richard Wagner described the Seventh as the 'apotheosis of the dance': 'All the violence, all the longing of the turbulent heart, here turns to joyous high spirits which sweeps us away with overpowering Bacchic force through every part of nature, through all the streams and seas of life, confidently rejoicing wherever we step out in the bold rhythm of this human dance of the spheres.'[138] Beethoven consistently follows the dance theme, with the tripping movement of a tarantella in the first movement and the measured tread of a procession of pilgrims in the second.[139] It is easy to pick out the dance element in the *Scherzo* movement, and the orgiastic frenzy described by Wagner appears in the finale. We should not, however, ignore the disciplined and fanfare-like subsidiary theme or the military rigour of the clipped rhythms, reminiscent of François Joseph Gossec's revolutionary march *Le Triomphe de la République*.

The Eighth Symphony is almost a satirical farewell to the genre, and not only because of its finale. Even the first movement is strange: the opening theme, unlike those of the other symphonies, presents itself from the first as a complete twelve bar statement, making one wonder how any composer could develop further ideas and import contradictions into such a self-contained structure. In fact the movement does lack consistent development; instead, all its ideas are abruptly juxtaposed. It is loving, reserved, passionate, wild and solemn, all at once.

It was long thought that the so-called Maelzel canon, WoO 162, named after Johann Nepomuk Maelzel, the inventor of the metronome, was an important draft of the second movement of the symphony, the *Allegretto scherzando* (quite quick and playful). According to Anton Schindler, an acquaintance and notoriously unreliable biographer of Beethoven, Beethoven composed this canon in the spring of 1812 at a sociable farewell dinner, setting the words 'Ta ta ta ta ta . . . lieber Maelzel, leben Sie wohl, sehr wohl! Banner der Zeit, grosser Metronom' (Tick, tick, tick, tick, tick . . . dear Maelzel, fare thee well, very well! Captor of time, great metronome'). However Maelzel did not yet present his invention to the public until 1816, and it seems that the canon is probably not even by Beethoven.

However, when Beethoven was composing the *Allegretto scherzando* he could well have been thinking of one of the mechanical musical instruments for which Maelzel was famous, and which he exhibited in his Kunstkabinett (cabinet of art) in Vienna. Admittedly the movement does not pursue a regular course like clockwork running down, despite what one might expect after hearing the first bars. But the music has a mechanistic quality, like a machine with a mind of its own: 'melody' and 'accompaniment' are not consistent, nor do they always fit together. There are overlaps, extensions, concentrations and distortions. Finally, the machine seems to break up, ending abruptly in a weird, self-propelled flurry of activity, as if someone has hit it to get it going again.

Like that movement, the next, described as *Tempo di Menuetto*, is

Even during his lifetime there were discussions whether Beethoven's metronome instructions for his music should be followed rigorously. Doubting voices argued that Beethoven used deficient metronomes. But Arnold Schoenberg and his pupils made a strong case in favour of Beethoven's original instructions; the pianist and musicologist Peter Stadlen proved that Beethoven's metronome notations should in most cases be taken seriously. The result of this, however, is that very often the pieces should be played at much quicker tempi than audiences were formerly accustomed to. But the controversy rumbles on, and the once-discussed suggestion that Beethoven had difficulty reading Maelzel's metronome accurately is gaining credibility.

anything but conventionally correct: one might be listening to an ensemble having some difficulty in playing properly together. The trumpets and timpani enter too early; the first violins begin hesitantly, and finally the timpani are two beats late, thus causing further uncertainty. The effects may be meant humorously, like the peasants' music in the third movement of the 'Pastoral' Symphony, but a certain sense of inward wrath is evident.

If we fit the finale into the picture as a whole we get an even stronger impression that in the Eighth Symphony Beethoven is expressing a fundamental scepticism towards his own high-flown idealism. The work is not a harmless joke but an expression of Romantic irony: the composer seems to be taking everything apart into its separate components and putting it together again wrongly, the aim (an unsuccessful one?) being to make us contemplate not ideal dignity and grandeur but wretched inadequacy.

It is no coincidence that Beethoven's contemporaries called him their musical Jean Paul.[140] To the novelist Jean Paul 'destructive humour' was an 'expression of scorn for the world', evoking 'that laughter wherein there is still pain and grandeur'.[141] Beethoven's humorously disguised despair of 'this absurd world' – words put into the composer's mouth by Bettine von Arnim in her letter of 11 August 1810 – keeps his high-flying idealism alive, but only in the form of a demand for something lost.

## 'Must it be? – It must be!'

# Years of isolation · 1816–1827

Where Beethoven's public reputation is concerned, the 'heroic' part of his life lasted until the Congress of Vienna of 1814–15. His outward success could not ameliorate Beethoven's increasing isolation from around 1812. Within a few years he lost his three old patrons, the men who had smoothed his way into the aristocratic society of Vienna two decades before, and had always seen past his brusque manners. Prince Kinsky died in 1812, Prince Lichnowsky in 1814 and Prince Lobkowitz in 1816. It is true that Archduke Rudolph, for whose enthronement as archbishop of Olmütz in 1820 Beethoven would compose the *Missa solemnis*, now took over from them, but despite his influence as a member of the imperial house, he was not someone who could open up new perspectives to an artist.

Even Beethoven's social and amorous contacts with aristocratic ladies could no longer be taken for granted. Therese von Brunsvik remained an important confidante; she and Beethoven read many books together in the years around 1816,[142] possibly

Beethoven in middle age

Therese von Brunswick

including Rousseau's *Julie, ou la nouvelle Héloïse*, the famous epistolary novel depicting sensual passion changing to a friendship of true minds – a reflection of Beethoven's own situation. After his encounter with the 'Immortal Beloved' in July 1812 showed no clear path to happiness, Beethoven was increasingly inclined to choose the path of renunciation. The personal journal, which he began keeping in the autumn of that year makes this clear from the very first entry. While in 1807, as quoted above, he was still able to sigh: *Only love – yes, only love can give you a happier life*, his remarks are now uncompromising: *Submission, deepest submission to your fate, only this can give you the sacrifices for this manner of service – oh hard struggle! . . . You must not be a human being, not for yourself, but only for others; for you there is no longer any happiness except within yourself, in your art – O God! Give me strength to conquer myself; nothing at all must fetter me to life.*[145]

Beside much everyday material his notebooks contain many quotations or freely copied paraphrases from writings in which the diarist seeks comfort and inspiration. He makes extensive mention of the *Rig Veda* and other works of Indian and Egyptian wisdom, of Homer's two great epics, Plutarch's Lives, Christoph Christian Sturm's *Betrachtungen über die Werke Gottes im Reiche der Natur* (Reflections on the Works of God in the Realm of Nature), which for a time was Beethoven's daily reading, works by Kant, Herder, Schiller, and the 'tragedies of fate' by Zacharias Werner and Adolf Müllner which were widely performed in Vienna at the time.

We could add to these works, most of which were in Beethoven's heavily annotated library with entries from the conversation books. The famous remarks *Socrates and Jesus were my models* and *The Moral Law within us and the starry firmament above! Kant!!!* date from 1820.[144] To Beethoven, Socrates probably symbolized the moral gravity of ancient philosophy, Jesus, the Christian doctrine of brotherly love, and Kant, the Enlightenment, the belief in reason. The conversation books for the same year contain a conversation with the man of letters, Friedrich August Kanne, about Plato's idea of the state, which had fascinated Beethoven since the period of the 'Eroica'; in 1826 he was discussing the three great Greek dramatists Aeschylus, Sophocles and Euripides with the violinist Carl Holz (1798–1868).

The ageing Beethoven wrestled with ever increasing intensity towards an understanding of God, through both Oriental and Western theology. Beethoven took both analytical and spiritual interest in such subjects; he copied out passages from Johann Friedrich Leuker's *Brahmanisches Religionsystem* (Brahman System of Religion) of 1797 and several times quoted from Kant's *Allgemeine Naturgeschichte und Theorie des Himmels* (General Natural History and Theory of the Heavens) of 1755, an authority from whom he obviously thought it was well worth learning. He was interested in the laws of the planets' movements, as well as speculation as to their material consistencies, inhabitants, flora and fauna.

Beethoven told the harp player Johann Andreas Stumpff, as they sat on a grassy bank during an excursion to the Helenenthal together in 1824: *Here, surrounded by these natural beauties, I often sit for hours on end with my senses revelling in the sight of the responsive and fertile children of nature. Here the majestic sun is not hidden from me by any mean ceiling made by human hands, for the blue heavens are the sublime roof over me. When I consider the sky in the evening, marvelling, and the army of bright heavenly bodies, suns or worlds eternally soaring within its confines, then my own spirit soars above them, millions of miles away as they are, to the original source from which all that is created flows and from which new creations will ever proceed. Sometimes, when I try to give form to my excited feelings in notes – ah, then I am dreadfully disappointed: I cast my soiled sheet of paper to the ground and am firmly convinced that no earthborn man can ever set down those heavenly images that hovered in happy hour before his excited imagination in music, words, paint or sculpture.*[145]

Beethoven's ideas, as recorded in his diary and the conversation books, are not merely the musings of an amateur philosopher. They reflect that, not surprisingly for a man now almost totally deaf, his world was to a great degree only mind and ideas. Many of these ideas were set almost directly to music, free of the arduous intervention of development or elucidation. That was certainly the case with the *Abendlied unterm gestirnten Himmel* (Evening Song under the Starry Sky) WoO 150, which appeared as a musical supplement to the *Wiener Zeitschrift für Kunst, Literatur, Theater und Mode* (Viennese Journal of Art, Literature, Theatre and Fashion) in 1820. A few weeks earlier Beethoven had read, in the same journal, the *Kosmologische Betrachtungen* (Cosmological Reflections) of Joseph Littrow, director of the Vienna Observatory. His reading of them led him not only to Kant, whose remark about the 'starry sky' he quotes from Littrow in the conversation books, but also to the composition of the song, which he obviously sent to the editor of the journal himself.

Beethoven not only used such intellectual activities to help him approach his old aim, *to understand the minds of the good and wise of every age,* but also to master his personal destiny. He had to repeatedly fight his way through the all-too-familiar conflict between his natural inclinations and his artistic vocation. If his stoical decision to favour his artistic mission had once been, as he saw it, voluntary, by now it seemed a desperate resolve affirming a lifestyle which his affliction had made necessity.

Resignation to his fate was never something that came easily to Beethoven. There is much to suggest that it took him a long time to get over his sorrow at parting from the 'Immortal Beloved'. In September 1816 Fanny Giannatasio noted down some remarks by Beethoven pointing almost unambiguously in that direction. 'Five years ago he had met someone with whom he would have thought it the highest happiness of his life to be more closely connected. But the idea was not to be entertained, it was almost impossible, a chimera. Yet he felt now just as he had on that first day. I have never been able to get it out of my mind, those were his words.'[146] On 8 May he wrote to Ferdinand Ries, asking him to give his regards to his wife: *Unfortunately I have no wife myself, there was only one woman for me, whom I suppose I shall never possess.*[147]

The period after 1812, his 'year of renunciation', found Beethoven in both physical distress and material difficulties. He wrote to Joseph von Varena in early 1813: *My health is not of the best, and through no fault of my own my situation otherwise is probably the least favourable of my life.*[148] A little later he was temporarily obliged to support *an unfortunate sick brother, together with his family,*[149] that is to say Kaspar Karl, even though since Prince Kinsky's death the income from Beethoven's pension had been at risk. His financial situation was particularly precarious just then on account of his poor management.

Nanette Streicher (1769–1833), who later concerned herself with his domestic arrangements, described the deplorable condition of Beethoven's wardrobe and linen: 'He had not only no good coat but

'This is not the first time that Beethoven's friends have taken his clothes during the night and laid down new ones in their place; he has not the least suspicion of what has happened and puts on whatever lies before him with entire unconcern.'
JOSEPH MAYSEDER, 1823

DOMESTIC ARRANGEMENTS

not even a whole shirt.'[150] Maynard Solomon suspects that a suicide attempt frequently if vaguely mentioned in earlier writings on Beethoven can be dated around 1813.[151] He also believes he has evidence that Beethoven was visiting prostitutes at this time, and expressed his feelings of guilt in diary entries such as the following: *Sensual pleasure without spiritual union is and remains bestial, after such pleasure one has no trace of noble sensation, but rather remorse.*[152]

Beethoven had lodged with some regularity at the house of Baron von Pasqualati (1777–1830), a music-lover and art collector, in the years 1804 to 1814, but thereafter often changed his lodgings after less than a year. Nonetheless, he was always making new resolutions to run a well-ordered household. He had taken his nephew Karl into his home early in 1818, and to give the boy a sense of domestic security he sometimes employed a house-keeper, a manservant and a tutor, but usually this never went beyond mere good intentions. Housekeepers, kitchenmaids and parlourmaids succeeded one another in rapid succession; some-times they were given notice within a week, or fled from their employer's unpredictable temper. It is as characteristic as it is tragi-comic that in a conversation book of 1820 Beethoven noted down the publication details of a new cookery book: *Siegle, M. Kath. Bavarian Cookbook 3 florins 34 crowns w.w.* (Wiener Währung, Viennese currency), *Regenspurg catalogue, at Tendler's bookshop by the Graben in the Trattener building.*[153]

The following extract from the same conversation book reflects Beethoven's typical everyday life:

*Savings on fine clothes, Wiplingerstrasse near waterproof hat shop.*

*Machai's new invention of a carriage safe from collapse of horses, in Pest at Kilian's bookshop. Printing paper 2 fl. w.w.*

*To think you had a lawyer in Prague and that Karl has been lured away by her for the second time.*

*Kerzmann no. 854 [in] own house from Weiburggasse to the Bastei.*

Entry by the journalist Karl Bernard, a friend: 'One must try one's luck. Let's try it for your nephew.'

Entry by his friend Franz Oliva: 'The housekeeper is coming tomorrow morning.'

Entry by an unknown hand: 'Today we admired the Symphonia Eroica, well played but the violins too weak. Not in the allegro.'

Entry by someone unknown: 'Pre-Adamites. – Why didn't you come to see Stieler [artist then painting Beethoven's portrait]? – The red [wine] at 3 gulden is better. – He's gained the rank of Economic Councillor. – like all Austrians? – He's been intriguing everywhere.'

Entry by Bernard: 'They are people who live only for pleasure.'

*Linen 3 ells – writing paper – candles, wax candles and half-wax candles – string the Schlemmer violin – lambskin – Wasserkunst Bastei no. 1268 and 1269, left of the Stiege lodgings. – coffee dish for housekeeper – canvas – Balbier earthenware crockery.*

Entry by the painter J C Stieler: 'The picture has to dry, when it's dry I'll write to you and see if you can give me another hour.'[154]

Beethoven was not always downtrodden by the minutiae of his domestic circumstances. In his first two decades in Vienna he was frequently guest or lodger with the families of his mainly aristocratic friends; the Beethoven scholar Maynard Solomon mentions the Lichnowskys, Brunsviks, Guicciardis, Deyms, Bigots, Erdödys, Malfattis and Brentanos.[155] After 1816, the family of Cajetan Giannatasio del Rio (1764–1828), to whose private school Beethoven sent his nephew, took over the task of looking after him for a while. The composer felt at ease in the company of the daughters of the house, Fanny and Anna, who were of marriageable age and full of admiration for their gifted artist, who sometimes appeared relaxed and gallant, sometimes distrustful and ill mannered. However, his distrust of Giannatasio's educational methods doomed the friendship to crumble after a couple of years. From time to time Beethoven asked Nanette Streicher, a former child prodigy pianist and now, with her husband, co-owner of a highly-regarded piano-making firm, for assistance with his domestic affairs. She obviously provided it, for in January 1818 Beethoven writes: *I am her debtor in so many ways that I often feel ashamed.* In June 1818 he writes ironically: *I beg you, write me something comfortable soon about the arts of cookery, laundry and sewing.*[156]

From the end of 1822 to May 1824, and again in the last four months before Beethoven's death, Anton Schindler, who had once been a member of the legal firm which Beethoven consulted, and was also a good musician, frequented his lodgings. He was principally helpful with day-to-day matters, negotiating with craftsmen and copyists, running errands, writing letters, and advising Beethoven on contractual issues. The conversation books show that Schindler was also interested in Beethoven's work, even given that, as was discovered a few years ago, Schindler added a whole series of his own 'remarks' to the conversation books after

A caricature of Anton Schindler

Beethoven's death, in order to present himself to posterity as more of an artistic confidant of the Master than he was.

Schindler's eager over-familiarity soon got on Beethoven's nerves; in a letter to his brother Johann of 19 August 1823 he complains of *that contemptible, despicable man.*[157] After the great concert of May 1824 he broke with Schindler, writing in plain terms to his self-appointed 'confidential unpaid secretary'[158] to say that their association could no longer continue, and adding: *But in general I have a certain fear that one day you will bring me great misfortune.*[159] Subsequently the violinist Carl Holz took Schindler's place. The fact that Schindler later returned to Beethoven's circle of intimate friends shows that he was difficult to replace. After Beethoven's death Schindler implied that he had been close to the composer for years. Subsequently generations of scholars have wrestled with the question of how many of the Master's remarks reported by him are authentic.

Friedrich Rochlitz, editor of the *Allgemeine Musikalische Zeitung* and an associate of the publishers Breitkopf & Härtel, set down his first impressions of the ageing Beethoven when he visited Vienna in the summer of 1822: 'Beethoven seemed pleased, but he was disturbed. And had I not been prepared in advance the sight of him would have disturbed me too. Not his neglected, almost wild physical appearance, not the thick black hair hanging in shaggy locks around his head or anything like that, but the way he looks in general. Think of a man of about fifty, small rather than middling of stature, but very powerful and sturdy, stocky, with strong bone structure, something like Fichte's but fleshier, and his face in particular is fuller and rounder: a red, healthy complexion; restless, flashing eyes, which when his gaze is fixed on you are almost piercing; his movements either hasty or none at all; in the expression of his face, particularly those eyes, so full of intellect and life, there is a mixture or sometimes an instant alternation of the heartiest benevolence and of nervousness; his whole bearing expresses the tension, then restless and anxious attentiveness of a deaf man with very sensitive feelings; now he throws out a glad and easy word, then immediately sinks into gloomy silence.'[160]

Rochlitz only published his *Letters From Vienna* some years later, as a literary document. Their reliability has been questioned, but he seems to have given an accurate enough idea of Beethoven's dominating features. We may doubt his memory of black hair, in view of the extant portraits of this time, but other sources confirm Beethoven's neglect of his outward appearance. It is even said that on one occasion he was arrested by the police because he looked like a tramp and was peering into strangers' windows in the Neustadt.[161]

However, Beethoven was sometimes well presented even now. In July 1822, on the occasion of another meeting in Baden near Vienna, Friedrich Rochlitz found Beethoven 'perfectly clean and neat, even elegant . . . Yet that did not prevent him (for it was a hot day) from taking off his fine black frock-coat on a walk in the Helenenthal, that is to say on the same route as is taken by everyone, even the Emperor and his noble family, and where people have to pass one another very close on the paths, which are mostly narrow, and then carrying it slung over his back by his stick, and walking along with his arms bare.'[162]

In the tavern Beethoven did not actually engage in conversation but talked 'on his own, and usually at some length, as if at random. Those with him added little, just smiled or nodded their approval. He talked philosophy and politics in his own way . . . He said all this without any care in the world or the slightest reservation, and it was all spiced with the most original, naïve judgements or delightful ideas.'[163] Rochlitz was reminded of a genius marooned from boyhood on a desert island, now a grown man, holding forth everything he had thought of and imagined in the intervening solitary years.

One cannot discuss Beethoven's personal relationships in the last twelve years of his life without considering a complex situation compared to which everything else was marginal: his tyrannical care for his nephew. In this relationship, and disastrously,

Beethoven lived out the still unresolved disappointments he had suffered with women. Fanny Giannatasio records a comment of Beethoven's of March 1816, when he said that he 'would never tie a holier knot than that now linking him to his nephew';[164] the composer was echoing the words in which Josephine Deym had tried to explain to him, years before, why her duty to her children kept her from being able to reciprocate his wooing. By now, apparently, Beethoven no longer hoped for freely given happiness, and could only attempt to possess an object to love through force.

The death of his brother Kaspar Karl in November 1815 opened up the way for Beethoven to acquire a family of his own. Maynard Solomon may be right in supposing that Beethoven was anxious to be close not just to his nephew Karl but also, subliminally, to his sister-in-law Johanna,[165] although we should be wary of too detailed a psychoanalytical interpretation. Above all, Beethoven wanted to be a loving father, better than any other father before him, his own included.

Beethoven's nephew Karl

The events themselves took a painfully long time, but can be summed up quite briefly; when Beethoven learned from his brother, on his deathbed, that Kaspar Karl's will made him Karl's joint guardian with his sister-in-law, he forced Kaspar to change it and name him as sole guardian. When Kaspar realized that he had thereby barred Johanna from bringing up her son, he added an extensive codicil expressly making it clear that he did not in any circumstances want Karl

KARL VAN BEETHOVEN

'to be removed from his mother'.[166] That did not prevent Beethoven from exerting all the influence he could to separate the child from Johanna.

At the beginning of 1816 the *Landrecht* court allowed him to take Karl into his household. On 6 February Beethoven wrote to Antonie von Brentano: *Meanwhile I have been fighting to tear a poor unfortunate child from an unworthy mother, and I have succeeded – te deum laudamus.*[167] He confided to the physician Karl von Bursy: *The boy must be an artist or a scholar if he is to live a higher life and not sink entirely into the common run. Only artists and scholars working freely carry their happiness within them.*[168] On 13 May he proudly told Countess Anna Maria Erdödy that he was a father: *For so I now regard myself.*[169] In his comment to his friend the lawyer and musical amateur Johann Nepomuk Kanka: . . . *I am the real, physical father of my dead brother's child,* he seems to be verging on delusion.[170] He did all he could to prevent mother and child from even seeing each other.

To justify this cruel conduct he constantly condemned Johanna for her immoral way of life, which made her unfit to bring up a child, even accusing her of prostitution. This line in a conversation book of 1820, *Born for intrigue, practised in deception, mistress of all the arts of dissimulation,*[171] is among his more moderate comments. Despite all his venomous tirades, there were also attempts at reconciliation, and he occasionally gave his sister-in-law financial support. When there was a rumour in 1820 that he was in love with Johanna his denial was expressed quite mildly.[172] Johanna conceived a child by Financial Councillor Johann Hofbauer, a girl born at the end of 1820, to whom she gave the name Ludovica. Before his death, when it was pointed out to him that by the terms of his will Johanna would be his heir after Karl, Beethoven expressly confirmed his approval.

First, however, there were a great many conflicts and dramatic outbursts. From the autumn of 1818 onwards the mother did all she could to get her son back. A first appeal to the courts failed, but when Karl ran away from school and was taken back by the police she managed to get the case re-opened. In the course of these proceedings Beethoven himself clumsily drew the court's attention to the fact that he bore no title of nobility. Thereupon the *Landrecht* (court restricted to the nobility) responsible for the nobility passed the case on to the civil courts for the middle classes – a 'degradation' from which Beethoven never recovered, and one that drove him to re-doubled efforts to be enobled.

The Viennese civil court was obviously more alienated than impressed by Beethoven's statements, which were certainly rather strange, and gave custody of Karl to his mother. Thereupon, Beethoven turned to the court of appeal, and after much tedious business he did in fact get what he considered justice in July 1820: *For I am a man hunted on all sides like a wild beast, misunderstood, often treated in the lowest way by this vulgar authority; and with all my other cares, I must always contend with that monster of a mother* – it was in such terms that he wrote to his lawyer, in a 48-page memorandum.[173]

In the following years matters calmed down, or so at least it seemed. Karl spent four years at Joseph Blöchinger's school for boys, and went to the Polytechnic Institute in 1823. Having become accustomed to his 'father's' tyrannical love, he made himself indispensable at home, and appears, despite Beethoven's suspicious and educationally narrow-minded nature, to have been a sensible, respectful and even affectionate nephew – at least his remarks in the conversation books suggest as much. They do however also include Karl's request to Beethoven of November 1826: 'If you want to go away, fine – if you don't, that's fine too – only please let me ask you once again not to torment me so. You may be sorry in the end; I can endure a good deal, but not what is too much.

That's what you said to your brother today, and for no good reason; you must remember that other people are human beings too.'[174]

Earlier, on 30 July 1826, Karl attempted to shoot himself in the head, but suffered only a slight wound. At the police examination he said, logically enough: 'I became worse because my uncle wanted me to be better.'[175] Carl Holz took Beethoven the unsparing message: 'He will give no reason except that he feels he is in prison with you.'[176] In line with the customary regulations, the failed suicide was sentenced to six weeks of religious instruction in police custody upon his recovery. Beethoven and his friends succeeded in getting him into a regiment in Iglau in January 1827 to do his military service; after he had finished, Karl led what appears to have been a normal life as a private citizen. He may have felt that the death of his 'father' barely eight months after his suicide attempt came as a release.

Biographers have always pointed out that the years 1816 to 1819 were extraordinarily unproductive in Beethoven's work, and have supposed that the protracted proceedings over his nephew made it difficult for him to concentrate. But in a man so able to focus his entire life onto his art, it seems just as plausible to switch cause and effect round and wonder whether Beethoven's creative crisis came first, and his obsessive concern for his nephew was an attempt at self-therapy.

Beethoven's creativity was in part a reaction to his own feelings. But his attempt to express unfulfilled human wishes in elevated music had failed him as a person. His music did not gratify or even silence his longings for love, harmony, and family security, which had lived in him since childhood. It is telling that he completed the Eight Symphony, with its ironical departure from the affirmative heroic style, at a time when he was writing his letters to the

'Immortal Beloved' – letters full of passion but tending towards renunciation.

The 'heroic manner' had not been politically topical since the Congress of Vienna. Beethoven's cantata composed in 1814, *Der glorreiche Augenblick* (The Glorious Moment) Op 136, begins with the optimistic words: 'Europa steht!' (Europe stands firm). It soon became clear, however, how and where Europe would stand in the years that followed. The old-established European princes, restored to power, had no intention of granting freedom to those who had fought and shed blood for them. Instead, a now notorious era of reaction followed, and the Karlsbad Agreements of 1819 set the seal on it. Beethoven was driven to resignation and political despair; where were there any ideals worth supporting now that the fight for liberty, first with and then against Napoleon, had led to such sad consequences? During Napoleon's Hundred Days, the period between his escape from Elba and the battle of Waterloo, during which Napoleon briefly resumed rule of France, Beethoven wrote to Kanka: . . . *how am I to serve them with my art, they say . . . do they want the conversation with himself of a king who has fled* [Louis XVIII] *or the perjury of a usurper* [Bonaparte] *celebrated in song?*[177]

*The most wretched of everyday and unpoetic scenes surrounds me – and makes me morose*, he complained in July 1815 to Joseph Xaver Brauchle. Later he expressed himself strongly about the consequences of the Restoration ushered in by the Congress of Vienna. In January 1820 he retrospectively praised Napoleon; according to Beethoven, only his hubris had brought him to grief: *He had a mind for art and science, and hated darkness. He should have valued the Germans more and protected their rights . . . But he overthrew the feudal system everywhere, and was the protector of right and the law.*[178]

Such opinions were dangerously tantamount to treason, and Beethoven's friends constantly warned him against speaking out too frankly and too loudly in public. In March 1820 Karl Bernard noted, in one of the conversation books: 'Czerny has told me that the Abbé Gelinek was speaking very angrily against you in the Camel [restaurant]; he said you were a second Sand [the assassin], that you abused the Emperor, the Archduke, the ministers, and would end on the gallows yet.'[175] The Bremen amateur musician Wilhelm Christian Müller commented on Beethoven's disrespectful language when he visited Vienna in autumn 1820: 'The police knew about it, but left him alone, whether as a fantasist or out of respect for his brilliant artistic genius.'[180]

The educational project which his nephew represented could almost have been devised by Beethoven on purpose in order to see his commitment to a heroic love of humanity rewarded, if only privately. The composer who had earlier depicted the deeds of Prometheus in his works now became a Prometheus himself, intending to shape a new and happy version of mankind in the person of his unfortunate nephew. His reading of Rousseau may have persuaded him that it was worth emulating not only the change from passionate love to intellectual friendship but also Rousseau's utopian ideas of education.

While his commitment to his nephew, certainly until the fateful pistol shot, may have appeared outwardly successful, it was doomed to failure. He would neither succeed in creating a new human being or pure love between 'father and son'. As time went on, Beethoven must have sensed more and more strongly that he could not get the happiness he longed for by force, even through a heroic educational struggle. And it was that insight that enabled him to compose again after the fallow period. Beethoven now appears far from a conqueror accustomed to victory, but as a man who must struggle hard for humanity in the Ninth Symphony, who must strive to find inner and outer peace even after the final chord of the *Missa solemnis*, and who finally, in the last quartets, overcomes all the fragility of the world through acceptance and resignation.

The number of works of stature completed between 1816 and 1821 is small; those that should be mentioned in particular are the song cycle *An die ferne Geliebte* (To the Distant Beloved) and the piano sonatas Opus 101, 106, and 109 to 111, which have traditionally been regarded as a bridge to the late works. Also of outstanding importance is the '33 Variations for Piano on a Waltz by Diabelli', written in 1819 to 1823, known generally as the 'Diabelli' Variations, a work rightly ranked with Johann Sebastian Bach's *Goldberg Variations* and Robert Schumann's *Kreisleriana*. Maynard Solomon regards it as a 'gigantic cycle of bagatelles',[181] such as those presented under that name by Beethoven in his Six Bagatelles for Piano Op 126. They are essentially experimental 'music about music,' anticipating the explorations of the late string quartets.

Meanwhile, even greater works were in preparation. On 9 July 1817 Beethoven writes to Ferdinand Ries: *I shall be in London in the first half of the month of January at the latest. The two great symphonies, entirely newly composed, will be ready then.* Beethoven never made it to England, nor did he compose these two symphonies by this self-imposed deadline, but during the following year he was writing down detailed ideas for new symphonic compositions in a sketchbook, ideas gradually making their way towards a D minor symphony with a choral finale, a setting of Schiller's 'Ode to Joy' – what would become his Ninth Symphony. This was a project that had returned to Beethoven's mind again and again ever since his early days in Bonn. There is clear evidence that the symphony was at the planning stage in 1822, and this project came to fruition in the two following years.

Beethoven's work on the *Missa solemnis* began in 1818; at first it appeared to be a straightforward commission, but when the

Mass was not completed at the appointed time it grew into a more substantial work. It is among the typical contradictions of Beethoven's life that the sale of this 'work close to his heart' was accompanied by unedifying bargaining with half a dozen publishers, and ended with a rift from his long-time friend and tireless supporter Franz Brentano.

Although Beethoven was living a retired life in the years after the Congress of Vienna, always complaining to his visitors of insufficient public recognition, he was not forgotten by the city that had once bestowed on him citizenship and exemption from taxation. In the years 1816 to 1818 he regularly took part in the Streichers' evening piano recitals, and in the following years he sometimes moved audiences by improvising on the piano at Carl Czerny's private Sunday recitals. He occasionally conducted one of his symphonies, particularly at charity concerts, and at the opening of the Josephstadt Theatre in the autumn of 1822 he conducted the overture *The Consecration of the House* Op 124. A little later the new production of *Fidelio* was a great success, although during rehearsals Beethoven was bitterly disappointed to find that his deafness no longer allowed him to conduct an ensemble.

He had been planning for years to travel to London, where his works were admired and frequently played by the Philharmonic Society. As he told Ferdinand Ries, he might escape *total ruin* through them, and on 20 December 1822 he was sighing: *If I were only in London, what would I not write for the Philharmonic Society!*[182]

It can have been no secret to his close friends and admirers that Beethoven's music sometimes seemed to be more popular abroad than at home in Vienna. Consequently, when there was talk of a new symphony, perhaps to be performed in Berlin, 30 Viennese musicians, publishers and enthusiasts appealed to the composer in a little memorandum: 'Do not deny the public, distressed as it is for want of what is great and perfect, enjoyment of the performance

Beethoven out and about in Vienna. Drawings by P Lyser

of the latest masterpieces from your hand. We know that a great sacred composition has now joined that first one in which you immortalized the sensations of a soul penetrated and transfigured by the power of faith and by the light of the supernatural. We know that a new flower blooms brightly in the garland of your beautiful and still unequalled symphonies.'[183]

Beethoven was touched, and agreed to give a concert that, for the first time in many years, was again to be an outstanding public

THE LAST CONCERT

occasion – and also his last concert before his death. On 7 May 1824 the overture Op 124, the Kyrie, Credo and Agnus Dei from the *Missa solemnis* and the Ninth Symphony were performed at the Kärntnerthor Theatre. The three extracts from the Mass were advertised as 'Hymns', since movements from a Mass should really have been performed only in a sacred context. Top-ranking musicians who also admired Beethoven took part: the singers Henriette Sontag and Caroline Unger, Schuppanzigh

as leader of the orchestra, and Kapellmeister Michael Umlauf. The final applause was tremendous. Caroline Unger made the composer, who was sitting deep in thought, stand to acknowledge the plaudits; he bowed, but his deafness prevented him from being able to participate fully in the general enthusiasm.

On this occasion – a triumph, albeit one praised chiefly by those who already admired his work – Beethoven unfortunately could not lay aside his now habitual distrust of those who helped him or refrain from making many

Henriette Sontag (1806–54), who also sang the soprano part in the first performance of the Ninth Symphony

brusque remarks. The atmosphere afterwards, therefore, was not good. Indeed, after a second and less successful performance of the works on the programme the composer, disappointed by the low takings, expressed a suspicion that he had been cheated financially. His agitation was understandable. At this time he owed money to friends and publishing houses, since the income from his pensions and publishing royalties was not enough to maintain his present high standard of living (he usually employed two servants and had his nephew to maintain), and he did not want to touch his bank shares, valued at about 10,000 gulden, wishing to bequeath them in their entirety to his nephew.

Whilst financial success eluded Beethoven at least the world at large recognized him. When he was appointed a member of the Royal Swedish Academy in 1823, he was anxious to have the news published in the Viennese press. He reacted with delight to the gift of a gold medal from King Louis XVIII of France; he sent Prince Galitzin a copy and told him proudly that this fine piece weighed *half a pound in gold*. His fervent wish to be properly honoured by the king of Prussia, to whom the Ninth Symphony is dedicated, was granted rather unsatisfactorily just before his death: the 'diamond ring' sent to him instead of the order he was expecting turned out to contain a not very valuable reddish stone, and the disappointed Beethoven immediately wanted to sell it. When the violinist Carl Holz objected that the ring was, after all, a king's gift, he replied very much in his old style: *I am a king too*.[184]

Even during his work on the Ninth Symphony, Beethoven had begun sketches for the String Quartet in E Flat Op 127. This was the first of three quartets commissioned by Prince Galitzin, and was completed in February 1825; Beethoven concluded the Quartet in A Minor Op 132 in July of that year. At his publisher's request, Beethoven replaced the concluding fugue of the Quartet in B Flat Op 130, completed in November, with a more accessible fast movement. Since Beethoven hardly ever went entirely against his artistic convictions, it is at least possible that he did not mind the separate publication of the *Grosse Fuge* as Op 133 too much; in its mixture of the elevated, the powerful and the expressive, the movement is indeed grandiose, but in the context of the last quartets, which, though rugged too, are full of subtle and fast-moving impressions, it stood out like a monolith.

In 1826 the quartets in C Sharp Minor Op 131 and in F Op 135 followed. The closing movement of the latter bears the superscript title *A decision made with difficulty*, followed by the musical motto: *Muß es sein? – Es muß sein!* (Must it be? – It must be!). Whether we see this motto as an innocent joke, the expression of grim humour, or a line drawn under the composer's life's work, it does in fact mark the end. The only exception is the replacement finale to the String Quartet in B flat Op 130, which Beethoven finished on the country estate of his brother Nikolaus Johann at Gneixendorf near Krems, where, already severely stricken by his nephew's suicide attempt, he fell dangerously ill in November 1826.

He complained of pain in his lower body, loss of appetite and thirst. During his journey back to Vienna in the company of Karl, his condition deteriorated. The physician called in, Dr Andreas Wawruch, found him in his lodgings in the Schwarzspanierhaus 'afflicted with severe symptoms of inflammation of the lungs. His face glowed, he spat blood, his respiration threatened suffocation, and a painful stitch in his side made lying on his back a torment.'[185] After a temporary improvement, the liver disorder which was really responsible for his serious condition entered its final phase. His swollen lower torso was drained of fluid several times, but without any real success. The many friends and colleagues who visited him guessed that they were looking at a dying man.

His friend Dr Malfatti advised giving the patient chilled wine to alleviate the pain and cheer his often troubled mind. At this Beethoven asked the publisher Schott in Mainz to provide *some very good old Rhine wine*. On 1 March 1827 he repeated this wish, and then dictated to Schindler: *A few days ago, on 27 February, I had my 4th operation, but I cannot yet look forward to complete improvement and a cure.*

On 24 March Beethoven was given the sacraments: on the same day Anton Schindler told the pianist Ignaz Moscheles: 'He feels his end approaching, for yesterday he said to me and Herr von Breuning: *Plaudite amici, comoedia finita est.'* ('Friends, applaud. The comedy is finished.')[186] Beethoven died late in the afternoon of 26 March 1827, as a thunderstorm broke over Vienna. His sister-in-law Johanna and the composer Anselm Hüttenbrenner, a friend of Schubert, were present at his deathbed.

Dr Johann Wagner's post-mortem report indicates that the cause of death was cirrhosis of the liver: 'The liver appeared shrunk to half its volume, almost like

Was Beethoven's excessive consumption of alcohol, which led to the cirrhosis of his liver and ultimate death, a habit inherited from his alcoholic father? Or should one follow Maynard Solomon, a Beethoven scholar influenced by psychoanalysis, and build a 'matrix of family circumstances, actions, and attitudes' as an explanation for this personality trait? Both theories lead one into contradictions and difficulties. Sometimes it may be better to let the phenomena stand in their strangeness rather than insist on too quick an explanation to iron out every problem. *Beethoven's Hair* by Russell Martin (Bloomsbury, 2000) tells the whole story,

Beethoven's death mask

DEATH

leather, greenish blue in colour, and with nodules the size of beans all over its lumpy surface and in its substance; all its vessels were very narrow, thickened and bloodless.'[187]

In a secret drawer, Beethoven had hidden the bank shares mentioned above, his letters to the 'Immortal Beloved' and a medallion bearing a stylized portrait of a woman, which some have tried to identify with her. Auction of his effects raised 1440 gulden, 18 kreuzer.

We are told that some twenty thousand people assembled outside the Schwarzspanierhaus at three in the afternoon on 29 March for the funeral. The coffin was taken to the parish church in Alsergasse; eight Kapellmeisters held the sides of the pall, and musicians walked as torchbearers on both sides. One of them was Franz Schubert. Since no speaking was allowed during the burial in the Währing cemetery, the funeral oration, written by the poet Franz Grillparzer, was delivered at the entrance gate, where the coffin was put down.

# The late works

There are two major watersheds in Beethoven's creative work. Shortly after 1800 the composer set out on what he himself called a *new path*. He came to regard each work he composed as an autonomous art work making its unique contribution to a musical philosophy. The style of many of these works has led to this being called the 'heroic' period, and it is also neo-classical in a more general sense; moral victory appears as the triumph of form. Everything is put to the service of the fine and elevated style that organizes, transfigures and idealizes. The finales of the symphonies and overtures announce a collective victory, the piano sonatas express the individual's self-conquest. The opera *Fidelio* presents similar ideas very distinctly through the medium of dramatic action.

Admittedly, the music of this period is by no means as consistently idealistic and neo-classical as for instance, the Fifth Symphony; such striking works as the Piano Sonata Op 31 No 2 or the Third 'Eroica' Symphony can be restless and fantastic, both in form and ideas. But Beethoven was still trying to control that potential. Not until the symphonies of 1812 is there a clear change; the triumphant ending of the Seventh is more like an explosive release than a final concentration of power, and the Eighth distinctly expresses the impossibility of a heroic solution.

After the Eighth Symphony, there followed a long fallow period that lasted right up to the composition of the late quartets in the mid-1820s. At first Beethoven concealed his creative difficulties by composing the rather conventional works commissioned for the Congress of Vienna. After that, it became obvious that he no longer took victory for granted. He gave himself up instead to a new stage of experimentation.

After a preliminary attempt in the Cello Sonata Op 102 No 2, in the 'Hammerklavier' Piano Sonata Op 106 (composed between 1817 and 1819) Beethoven experimented with a closing fugue, entitled *Allegro risoluto* (lively and resolute), a clear echo of Johann Sebastian Bach.

Here, at the close of this mighty sonata – *which is to be my greatest*, Beethoven told his pupil Czerny[188] – Beethoven demonstrated the power of traditional musical techniques to convey emotion. The result, full as it is of technical difficulties, is impressive and as forceful as it is mysterious. Beethoven's attempt to do the same in the Piano Sonata Op 110, composed in 1821, the year of Josephine Brunsvik's death, is of still greater persuasive power. With the help of Beethoven's directions written above the score, we can trace the sonata's expression of a poetic idea. Words such as *Moderato cantabile molto expressivo* (in a moderately 'singing' style with much expression) and, more specifically, *con amabilità* (with love) and *sanft* (gently) suggest the feelings being conveyed.

What could be defined in formal theory as the main theme is only a motto, a sigh that breaks off after being heard twice at the beginning and leads into a trill. This 'sigh' is obviously too personal to be manipulated; even in the development it is not changed, only quoted now and then. Beethoven uses this motto to suggest his idea of pure, ideally transfigured femininity in a lyrical 'flow of feelings'.[189] The words 'Liebe Josephine' (Dear Josephine) can be read into the notes and rhythm of this motto. Whether or not we take this as a subtle but heartfelt tribute to Josephine von Brunsvik, the motto can be seen as a personal, if not exactly a private, statement.

The second movement of the sonata, in the brusque manner of a *scherzo*, is less emotional. But open complaint breaks out in the third movement. The song-like expressiveness of the music is no longer confined to a coded motto, but expands into a recitative that leads into an *Arioso dolente* (lamenting song).

The music moves from the sad key of A flat minor into the lighter regions of the major in the closing fugue, which, unlike the close of the 'Hammerklavier' Piano Sonata Op 106, has a comforting beauty. We can see what is happening, both in the context of the sonata, and in its connections with Beethoven's life. The original structure of the theme changes the pleading tone of the opening motto into confidence; its inversion, after a new but now subdued lament, anticipates the prayer for peace ('Dona nobis pacem') from the *Missa solemnis*, on which Beethoven was already working. What began in the first movement as a sigh of longing ends, after a deeply felt lament, with a sense of greater insight that nonetheless preserves the expression of grief that has gone before. As a whole, the sonata has the elevated tone characteristic of the neo-classical period, but it is far from heroic. The message is not of victory but of resignation – and that resignation can only be achieved through endurance.

These fugal finales of the sonatas, the Cello Sonata Op 102 No 2 and the Piano Sonatas Op 106 and Op 110, are not just an isolated episode in Beethoven's creative work, but represent a determined attempt to refashion the fugue, a musical form seen at the time as traditional and objective, into his own more subjective and poetic style. In his later years Beethoven expressly insisted that *something else, a truly poetic element must be added to the old, traditional form* of the fugue.[190]

Just as Beethoven's concern with the fugal tradition is character-istic of his major works in the period after 1818, so is his turn to vocal music. In the last movement of the Piano Sonata Op 110 it is only the melodic voice of the piano that 'sings'; the large-scale works written at the same time – the *Missa solemnis* and the Ninth Symphony – actually give vocal parts to chorus and soloists. In both cases part of the purpose of having a (sung) text is to overcome any doubts Beethoven felt as a purely instrumental composer.

This is obvious in the *Missa solemnis*. The traditional sacred text makes the meaning of the piece clear; in the work that he himself

Beethoven composing the *Missa Solemnis* by J C Stieler 1819

described as his greatest, Beethoven communicates not through symphonic writing, but through devout appropriation of the liturgy, for Beethoven told Andreas Streicher, on 16 September 1824, that *it was his main intention to arouse religious feelings in both the singers and those who heard the work, and make those feelings endure.*[191]

The words entered in the autograph score above the 'Kyrie' – *Von Herzen – Möge es wieder – zu Herzen gehn!* (From the heart – may it return – to the heart!) suggest how much the Mass relates to Beethoven's personal feelings. The entry in the 'Dona nobis pacem' (Give us peace), *Bitte um den innern und äussern Frieden* (Prayer for inward and outward peace), indicate this still more clearly. In a piano sonata performed by a single musician, this could be understood as an expression of individual resignation. In the monumental setting of the Mass, it is raised to a universal truth. One critic has commented on the Mass that 'dated, traditional, liturgical, dramatic and monumental elements sometimes [stand] almost unrelated side by side, but we also hear what moves subjectively "from heart to heart".'[192]

Beethoven returned periodically to his plans for new symphonies. On a sheet of paper containing sketches for the Piano Sonata Op 106 of 1818 he wrote: *Adagio Cantique – pious song in a symphony in the old keys – we praise thee, O Lord – alleluia – either on its own or leading into a fugue. Perhaps characterize the whole 2nd symphony* [meaning second of two he was

Beginning of the autograph manuscript of the Missa Solemnis.

FROM HEART TO HEART

then envisaging] *in this way, with the vocalists coming in at the end, or already in the adagio. The orchestra, violins, etc., to be ten times greater in the last movement. Or the adagio repeated in a certain way in the last movement, with the singers' voices coming in gradually – text in the adagio of the Greek myth, Cantique Eclesiastique – celebration of Bacchus in the Allegro.*[193]

This passage encapsulates the distinctive features of Beethoven after his 'heroic' period: a return to the old liturgical traditions, transcending personal confession, an interest in old styles, and an enthusiasm for hymnody, with, as the reference back to Greek mythology suggests, reminders of his neo-classical 'heroic' phase. These remarks illustrate the extent to which Beethoven thought through his music as a philosophical structure; naturally the tonal structure is also part of these preliminary ideas, but work on the intellectual conception takes precedence – at least in the Ninth Symphony, towards which the composer was making his way.

The Ninth Symphony, more than any other of Beethoven's compositions, must be not just heard, but understood as a philosophical work of art. If Beethoven was planning to compose a new symphony after a break of ten years – when the Eighth could have been interpreted as a farewell to the symphonic genre – then we must start by assuming that he was not simply planning to go on from where he had left off. The stakes were much higher.

It is extraordinary that Beethoven would write three movements of a symphony with the traditionally constructed opening, *Scherzo* and *Adagio* movements, and then present the choral setting of Schiller's 'Ode to Joy', without further comment, as a new kind of finale. It is as if this startling last movement – as Richard Wagner scathingly remarked to Franz Liszt – 'naively reveals the difficulty encountered by a composer who does not know, in the last resort, how to depict paradise (after hell and purgatory).'[194]

The extended fourth and final movement begins with what

Wagner called a 'fanfare of alarm'. Earlier drafts of the score include words (omitted from the final version) alongside the music. In the Landsberg 8 sketchbook, after the fanfare come the words: *Heute ist ein Feierlicher Tag . . . dieser sey gefeiert durch* [ . . . ] *Gesang u. Tanz* (*This is a solemn day . . . let it be celebrated in song and dance*).[195] Then the music runs back over the themes of the first three movements. The verbal commentary on the opening of the first movement runs: *No, not this, something else is what I require*. The *Scherzo* too is rejected: *Nor this, these are mere pranks . . . something merrier . . . finer and better*. The reminiscence of the *Adagio* does not meet with approval either: *Not this either, it is too delicate, one must look for something livelier, like . . . I will sing you something myself, and you join in*. The comment on the opening of the 'Joy' melody that follows runs: *Ah, this is it. Joy has been found . . .* In the definitive score, the 'Joy' melody performed unaccompanied by cellos and double basses develops into a mighty round performed by the chorus and soloists and combining such heterogeneous elements as a raucous Turkish march and a double fugue.

There has been much critical speculation on the meaning of the entire sequence. This author, who has taken part in the discussion himself, would like to make another and very simple suggestion which may complement points previously made. Beethoven writes the first three movements of a 'traditional' symphony on the highest musical plane available to him. In the first movement he looks back to his heroic period but intensifies the monumental and primeval factor; in the second, he intensifies the idea of the *Scherzo* into something wild and Bacchic; the *Adagio* sets new standards of contemplative inspiration. The hearers of this 'new' symphony increasingly come to feel that the Master has surpassed himself yet again. But before they can express their praise, he begins a finale questioning all that has gone before. The best symphonic music that can be played to humankind will fail before the real terrors to which humanity is exposed. He must see to his *own* salvation, and that will come if he joyfully and devoutly joins the song uniting all men as brothers under the sky of God, the father and creator.

Is this the real, final meaning of the symphonic thinking developed by Beethoven from the beginning of the century onwards, the ultimate conclusion of his wisdom? In *Dr Faustus*, Thomas Mann (1875–1955) makes his composer Adrian Leverkühn, faced with paralytic collapse, reject the Ninth Symphony as a symbol of deceptive idealism. By rejecting it, he rejects faith in what is good and noble: 'What men have fought for, what they have stormed citadels for, what the fulfilled have announced, rejoicing, shall not be. It will be taken back. Through my work I shall take it back.'[196]

This is a modern kind of pessimism. But one imagines the deaf Beethoven himself, clumsy and disorientated, bowing to the applauding audience at the première of the Ninth and wondering what he personally knew of the force of human solidarity he was praising in his symphony. If the Ninth Symphony had been his last composition, we might dismiss this as speculation. But in fact we have the late string quartets, which fascinatingly make it clear that Beethoven was not content with the triumph of an idea by which he himself could no longer live. Instead, he cast himself back upon the waters, making for banks scarcely perceived.

The 'new path' taken by Beethoven here is almost more breathtaking than the one upon which he set out barely quarter of a century before. It is so unique that it is a path hardly followed at all, for all his successors' veneration of him. In the late quartets, music no longer fits into the system of rules prescribed for it; it frees itself from its own laws. On the one hand the late quartets are composed on the basis of what was understood at the time as music – or more precisely as the music of Beethoven: the traditional sequence of movements is respected, or at least the idea

Beethoven in later years, by Karel le Dake

of it is not abandoned. The first movements allow sonata form structure to show through, and there are plenty of movements with the character of a *Scherzo*, an *Adagio* or a finale. Metre, harmony, melody and thematic development sometimes exhibit traditional, sometimes more unconventional features, but can almost always be traced back to the usual basic pattern. The key structure, despite making extreme demands on the instrumentalists, is quite traditional.

FREUDE

But the real innovation of the late quartets lies far from the surface. Beethoven's divergence from formal conventions is not so important as is his refusal to pay tribute to beauty of form in itself. Beethoven plays with form and deprives it of its authority. Instead of using it to control his material, he makes form the material itself. He denies his listeners the satisfying sense of actively participating in something universal. For that reason their perception of what is new becomes sharper.

The String Quartet in A minor Op 132 illustrates this tendency well. The opening movement certainly follows the pattern of a traditional sonata but it reveals its expressive content only if we hear it as one long 'sigh'. Typically, this penetrating lament is presented again and again, surrounded by difficult and original musical ideas. Rather than there being a sensitive balance, nerves are exposed. The following *Minuet* and *Trio* is far from the usual conventions of the genre: its main theme takes up the lament of the first movement and modulates it hesitantly into the major. The silvery, almost ethereal sound of the *Pastorale* with which the *Trio* opens and later closes moves into an ordinary 'German dance' which sounds like a brief passage from one of the many dances written by Beethoven for the Redoutensaal balls in Vienna. This move from the ethereal to the terrestrial poses semantic riddles.

*Aldous Huxley on the String Quartet Op 132*
Slowly, slowly, the melody unfolded itself. The archaic Lydian harmonies hung on the air. It was an unimpassioned music, transparent, pure and crystalline, like a tropical sea, an Alpine lake. Water on water, calm sliding over calm; the according of level horizons and waveless expanses, a counterpoint of serenities. And everything clear and bright; no mists, no vague twilights. It was the calm of still and rapturous contemplation, not of drowsiness or sleep. It was the serenity of the convalescent who wakes from fever and finds himself born again into a realm of beauty. But the fever was 'the fever called living' and the rebirth was not into this world; the beauty was unearthly, the convalescent serenity was the peace of God. The interweaving of Lydian melodies was heaven. *Point Counter Point*, 1928

The title, *Hymn of Thanks to the Deity from a Man Recovered from Illness, in the Lydian mode,* leaves no doubt about the intention of the following and unusually extensive *Adagio* movement. The very first note conjures up the world of the traditional archaic chorale, with the line-by-line development of a *cantus firmus,* in an intimate string setting. After the first verse of the chorale, the scene changes; with the performance direction *Feeling new strength* the composer, now using his own modern tonal language, pours a wonderful mixture of energy and tenderness into the concept of 'revival'. Considering the real situation of the composer, who had just recovered from severe illness, we may well feel moved, and admire the achievement of the spirit despite all the weaknesses of the body.

This sense of wordless song and speech is also present in the two closing movements, which merge into each other. A laconic little march leads into a rhythmically free recitative: the first violin acts like a diva in a dramatic scene, and the other strings accompany it *tremolo.* This is immediately followed by the aria, marked *Allegro appassionato* (lively and impassioned) and fully living up to that description. The quartet ends neither with triumph nor with reconciliation, but in a state of agitation: passion has not been assuaged.

The *Hymn of Thanks Adagio* movement is often regarded 'as the most remarkable piece of music that Beethoven ever wrote'.[197] However, it seems unusually mysterious only to those who will not allow that Beethoven was no longer seeking for harmonious equilibrium between personal experience and artistic expression, but was rather letting them clash harshly. The fundamental change in his musical aesthetic is this; 'life' no longer has to be conquered by or sublimated in art. If life is open-ended, inconsistent and contradictory, so too must be art.

Richard Wagner saw the String Quartet in C Sharp Minor Op 131,

often called the twin to Op 132, as 'the picture of a day in the life of our saint', a way of approaching Beethoven's world and ideas. Wagner, that musical freethinker, did not intend a reductive interpretation. Instead, he saw that Beethoven, rather than using music to describe the realities of his everyday life, allows his inner, subjective experience to permeate his art.

Page from manuscript of the second movement of the String Quartet Op 131. The staves have been drawn freehand.

In Wagner's interpretation the work, which with its unusual seven movements already invites inquiry as to its meaning, begins with the melancholy awakening to a day 'which will not fulfil a single wish throughout its long course, not one!' Thereafter the artist, 'his eye turned inward' seeks various places in his mental landscape 'as if he were listening to the sound proper to those phenomena that move before him in a rhythmic dance, first ethereally, then of the earth. He looks at life, and seems to remember at first striking up the tune of life itself like a dance: there is a short but sad moment of reflection, as if he were sinking into the deep dream of his soul. A glance has shown him the interior of the world again; he wakes, and now, in the finale, touches the strings in the music of such a dance as the world has never heard. This is the dance of the world itself; wild desire, sad lamentation, the delights of love, the heights of bliss, grief, rage, lust and suffering.' The composer thus becomes 'the minstrel of necessity holding all spellbound, proud and confidently leading from the vortex to the maelstrom, to the abyss; he smiles at himself, for to him this enchantment was only a game'.[198]

The music theorist, sociologist and philosopher Theodor Adorno (1903–69), the very opposite of Wagner in musical aesthetics but also an admirer of the late Beethoven, complements the picturesque terminology of maelstroms and abysses in his own way; to him, Beethoven's late style shows 'a tendency to dissociation, disintegration, dissolution' – not of course because of creative failings, but as an 'artistic method'.[199] But acute as this is, it is not the whole truth. Adorno himself contributed to the view that Beethoven's last works, more even than his earlier work, present a philosophy in music that is unlike almost anything else and does not need such a negative explanation.

'The higher the great geniuses soar, the further out of reach of those who claim they are created for them. This is especially so in music and dramatic literature. The other day I heard one of Beethoven's last quartets. M. Baillot introduced it at one of his evenings. I was intensely curious to see what effect this extraordinary work would have on the audience. There were nearly three hundred there, and precisely six of us half dead with emotion – we were the only ones who did not find the work absurd, incomprehensible, barbarous. He soared into regions where one breathes with difficulty. He was deaf when he wrote this quartet (Op 131). For him, as for Homer, "the universe was clasped within his mighty soul." It's music for him alone, or for those who have followed this incalculable progress of his genius.'
HECTOR BERLIOZ, 1829

That philosophy could be summed up as the 'realism of love'. Beethoven's love for his own tormented creation, and with it all mankind, no longer wishes for artistic constraint and harmonization. It must be tolerated in its disparity and yet do love's work. That work is neither self-contained nor incomplete, neither unified nor fragile, neither a psychic portrait nor an objective structure, and it suggests neither weakness nor strength. Beethoven's late work offers us a complex glimpse of an artist's never-resting existence, with its experiences of happiness, unhappiness and all that remains unresolved.

'A part of European history'

# Beethoven's later influence

' The fair mouthpiece of music, heir and successor to the immortal fame of Handel and Bach, of Haydn and Mozart, has come to the end of his life, and we stand weeping by the broken strings of an instrument that has fallen silent.' So wrote Franz Grillparzer in his funeral oration, delivered by the actor Heinrich Anschütz to Beethoven's mourners as 'the representatives of an entire nation'. 'As Behemoth ploughs stormily through the seas, he soared above the confines of his art. From the cooing of the dove to the crash of thunder, from the most subtle interweaving of unique artistic methods to the awe-inspiring point where creation merges with the chaotic autocracy of natural forces at odds, he traversed and seized upon everything. He who comes after him will not continue his work but must begin again, for his predecessor ceased only where art itself comes to an end.'[200]

This is literary pathos, but Grillparzer's words would have fitted no one else, and indeed set out exactly what Beethoven meant to intelligentsia of his time. For one thing, he gave them the right to speak of national greatness in music. The awareness of musical history which had developed in the first third of the 19th century drew nourishment from Beethoven's strong personality: he ennobled music and made it into an art that could contribute to the philosophical, aesthetic and political discourse of its time, an art in no way inferior to philosophy and literature.

In the spring of 1828 Fanny Mendelssohn, then aged 22, wrote from Berlin about the performances of Beethoven's symphonies, and continued: 'Well, it means a step has been taken. We live in general in a time where extraordinary things are achieved in every way, and so they are in art, whether we admit it or not. The St Matthew Passion by Bach will certainly be performed this year under Schlesinger the Frankfurt choral director, Schelble has presented a part of Bach's B minor Mass to much acclaim, something is going on everywhere, every branch is rustling, you have to put your hands over your ears if you don't want to hear it!'[201] She speaks, unselfconsciously and in the same breath, of the rediscovery of the great old master Bach and the validation of Beethoven's philosophical works of art. What they shared was their intellectual ambition, building national identity and rebelling, narrow-mindedly or not, against the superficiality of 'salon' music and Italian opera.

In the eyes of his contemporary Grillparzer, Beethoven stood at the apex of a pyramid of classics, Haydn and Mozart its other

Beethoven's funeral procession. Watercolour by Franz Stöber

BEETHOVEN, HAYDN, MOZART

two points. The three's music could be described as 'classical' because it expressed humanist values; its themes were those of the Enlightenment and the age of Goethe; its forms elevated and sublimated such primarily human utterances as song and dance, or worked through intellectual structures such as the sonata form; its ideal of beauty was that of unity, perfection, harmony, consistency, purity, and the equilibrium of form and content.

Over and beyond these qualities, and without explicitly saying so, Grillparzer also saw Beethoven as the Romantic who would not bow to the classical ideal of beauty, but ultimately transcended the tension between regulating ideals and creative autonomy. Finally, he praised the all-encompassing breadth and universality of his art, which made later musicians hesitate, within certain genres, 'to do anything after Beethoven'.[202]

The young Franz Schubert confided such doubts to his friend Joseph von Spaun as early as 1815. A generation later Johannes Brahms (1833–97), who had yet to write his First Symphony, sighed: 'I shall never compose a symphony! You have no idea how people like me feel when they keep hearing such a giant marching behind them.'[203] In the symphonic genre, in particular, all 19th-century composers measured themselves against Beethoven. How and whether a 'victorious' finale could be credibly written in an age of dwindling idealism occupied the minds of all the great writers of symphonic music up to Gustav Mahler (1860–1911). The legacy of Beethoven was often inhibiting.

That legacy was at least influential in the understanding of form, by German composers in particular. Beethoven completed the paradigm shift from form to structure that had been on its way since the time of Johann Sebastian Bach. 'Form' was a pattern given to the composer in advance, one that he must flesh out; 'structure' was determined by thematic material and followed the meaning immanent in the work. In this sense Johannes Brahms was a model pupil of Beethoven, and the members of the second Viennese School, building on his work – Arnold Schoenberg (1874–1951), Alban Berg (1885–1935), Anton Webern (1883–1945) – were positive apostles of structure; many tendencies in very recent music can also be traced back to the structural thinking of Bach and Beethoven.

However, it is often forgotten that Beethoven's works achieve greatness through the interweaving of structure and message. Works such as the Fifth Symphony and the Piano Sonata Op 110 contain structural experiments, not for their own sake, but in the service of a poetic idea. Every musical structure tends towards abstraction, but that does not mean it necessarily escapes from meaning. While Mozart had contented himself in his developments with 'mingling the themes with each other in a masterly manner', the development of Beethoven's themes always had 'something definite to say'. Composers such as Felix Mendelssohn (1809–47) and Robert Schumann (1810–56) 'failed' by returning to development of a more formal kind.[204]

Beethoven's ability to say 'something definite' was brought out particularly clearly by Franz Liszt (1811–86) and Richard Wagner (1813–83), who both appropriated it for their own particular purposes. Both saw Beethoven as the founder of an age in which music could 'reflect spirit and feeling, the life and ideals of a society' more subtly than before.[205] Liszt's symphonic poems (one movement orchestral pieces dealing with descriptive subjects from mythology, history and so on) and Wagner's operas differ greatly from Beethoven in form, but they follow him as an artist concerned to express ideas – albeit that those ideas are expressed more directly in a literary text or action on stage. Their ways of confronting the spirit, rather than the letter of Beethoven's achievements were no less productive than those of Brahms.

Beethoven bust in the Capodimonte Museum, Naples

Romanticism's response to Beethoven should not be underestimated. In an essay of 1813, E T A Hoffmann (1776–1822), the Romantic writer and composer famed for his bizarre and uncanny stories, lets Beethoven's instrumental music lead him into the 'world of the immense and the infinite', and speaks of 'gigantic shadows which surge up and down, gradually closing in on us more and more and annihilating everything in us, except the torment of endless longing in which all the pleasure swiftly rising in tones of rejoicing sinks and perishes'.[206] Hoffmann is expressing his enthusiasm for the magical power of music in general, and for the new dimensions opened up by Beethoven in particular, the element of the fantastic, holding us spellbound by its arbitrary transcending of boundaries.

Beethoven's Romantic successors had difficulty in going beyond their admiration and finding their own fantastic style. The most successful was probably Robert Schumann who wrote, at the age of 18, a year after Beethoven's death: 'When I hear the music of Beethoven, it is as if someone were reading Jean-Paul aloud to me.'[207] But Schumann's gift was for fantasy on a small scale, and his most extensive piano work, the Fantasy in C Major Op 17, is, significantly, a tribute both overt and covert to Beethoven. Perhaps Gustav Mahler and Dmitri Shostakovich (1906–75) were the only composers to keep the spirit of the fantastic and Romantic Beethoven alive within the symphonic genre.

20th-century music, by its nature, preserved a distance from Beethoven's 'music of experience' and its idealistic horizon of thought,[208] but it took inspiration from his attempts to radically free musical material. Pierre Boulez (b.1925) spoke of the finale of the Seventh Symphony as the 'triumph of rhythm' and a premonition of the *Rite of Spring* of Igor Stravinsky (1882–1971).[209] The surfaces of Beethoven's work can be related to the timbres of new music, whilst the constant repetitions in the Sixth 'Pastoral' Symphony have much in common with minimalism.

Over and beyond his place in the history of composition, we must not lose sight of Beethoven's place in wider history. The comments of the French writer and music scholar Romain Rolland (1866–1944) in 1927, the centenary year of Beethoven's death, are typical: 'Every period has its own concept of humanity, has its Son of God and its own views: what it does and refrains from doing, the words it utters are the common property of millions. In Beethoven's entire being – in his way of feeling and experiencing the world, in his unique form of understanding and will, in the laws of his creativity, in his ideas in general as much as in his physical constitution and his temperament, he presents a part of European history.'[210]

The comments of Rolland, who according to his own account had been surrounded by the aura of Beethoven from childhood and used to dream of him, are fervent but not untypical of the enthusiasm for Beethoven which continued for generations not only among educated Germans but in Europe as a whole. Beethoven was a figure with whom one could identify: more than any other music, his works were understood to be the artistic manifestation *par excellence* of modern Western man's Faustian condition. Faustian, that is, as in Goethe's great epic of modernity; a never-resting search for truth, involving self-examination, confrontation with

Johann Wolfgang von Goethe (1749–1832) is one of the giant figures of world culture, successful as a poet, dramatist, novelist and scientist. Beethoven set several of Goethe's poems to music, as well as writing music for his tragedy *Egmont*. The two met in July 1812 while on holiday. Beethoven had loved Goethe's poetry since childhood and once said that his greatest ambition was to provide music for Goethe's *Faust*. Goethe admired Beethoven's music but famously branded him 'a wholly untamed character'.

fate, suffering, conquest and intellectualization.

At the same time Beethoven's music offers something more than the Faust myth and Goethe's drama; Victory. Without that victory Beethoven could never have become such a hero of Western culture. On the one hand there is his revolutionary and utopian fire, on the other the power of the music; nowhere, not in any play or painting, can victory after the conquest of doubts and obstacles be celebrated as well as in instrumental music unaccompanied by words. The overture to Goethe's *Egmont* Op 84 could make one forget the whole of the play: in Beethoven's music, the victory of freedom is general but not abstract, full of sensuous rejoicing yet not concrete.

That said, the quality in music that philosophers and writers of the Romantic era liked to describe as 'absolute', that is, its lack of any defined text or programme outside the music, does make it susceptible to ideological appropriation. The 'Eroica', to mention only the most outstanding example, has been drafted in to support many different causes. A Romantic enthusiastically looking to the bourgeois revolution of 1848 like Wolfgang Robert Griepenkerl, who wrote such dramas as *Maximilian Robespierre* and *Die Girondisten* (The Girondins – a political grouping in the French Revolution), saw Beethoven's work as heralding the 'most recent artistic epoch'. 'Art has ceased to be playful,' wrote another; it is 'no longer the bell tolling for a single individual but the great bell of nations echoing down the centuries.'[211] In 1872 the pianist and conductor

Hans von Bülow (1830–94), still flushed with enthusiasm after the victory of German troops over the French, arbitrarily rededicated the 'Eroica'. At the end of a performance with the Berlin Philharmonic he made a speech in which he opposed the 'delusive words: Liberty, Equality, Fraternity' to the 'positive motto: infantry, cavalry, artillery', and in line with that notion cried: 'With heart and mind, with hand and mouth, we musicians consecrate and dedicate that heroic symphony today ... to the brother of Beethoven, the Beethoven of German politics, Prince Bismarck!'

In 1914 the music historian Walther Vetter looked towards the First World War in an essay on the 'Eroica' that contrasts the vice of 'idleness, standing passively by' with the ethos of the symphony, which demands 'an elevated and more noble life'. In 1927 Alfred Rosenberg (1893–1946), principal ideologist of the National Socialist party then preparing to seize power, announced in the Nazi newspaper *Völkischer Beobachter*: 'We are living today in the "Eroica" of the German people.' It is not surprising that the pianist Elly Ney (1882–1968), an admirer of Adolf Hitler (1889–1945), quotes the comments of a dive-bomber pilot in 1942: 'After flying in an air raid I happened to hear the "Eroica" on the radio that evening. I felt very clearly that this music is the affirmation of our struggle, and sanctifies what we are doing.'

One of the ear trumpets designed by Nepomuk Maelzel for Beethoven lying on top of the manuscript of the 'Eroica'.

Conservative thinkers and writers who cannot so easily be connected with National Socialism

Max Klinger's statue of Beethoven in Leipzig's Gewandhaus

such as Eduard Spranger (1882–1963), Richard Strauss's librettist Hugo von Hofmannsthal (1874–1929) and Richard Benz (1884–1966) also claimed that Beethoven sanctified what they did. In the course of its history the labour movement also frequently called upon Beethoven, whom the composer Hanns Eisler (1898–1962) called 'citoyen'. On 18 March 1905, for instance, a performance of the Ninth Symphony by 3000 Berlin workers was given in memory of the revolution of 1848, with reference to the humanist and progressive tradition in which the music stood. The Social Democrat art critic and cultural politician Heinrich Wiegand praised Beethoven in 1927 as a man 'who never avoided battle; creatively overcame the most profound misery; was outdone by no one in energy; the Last Things of mankind and an acute awareness of political and social events moved with equal vigour in his heart, where liberty, the brotherhood of man and death resounded in the most wonderful manner.' More recently Beethoven's Ninth Symphony has been chosen as the anthem of the European Union.

The majority of Beethoven's admirers understand his work less as a vehicle for ideology than as a kind of myth, complex, requiring interpretation, but offering real value and meaning.

Beethoven the man blurs into legend. He himself described his life as that of a warrior, patient sufferer, in the service of higher things. As artist and as human being, he offered the ideal realization of the 'power and purity' which Hugo von Hof-mannsthal wished to see in his people.[212] The German poet Richard Dehmel (1863–1920) wrote about the statue of Beethoven in Leipzig's Gewandhaus: 'Beside me sat Zeus, a new Zeus in the likeness and form of Beethoven, and his creative glance looks down from the throne of sin and redemption into the chasms of the world and mankind, while the eagle at his feet ruffles its plumage expectantly.'[213]

In the present author's view it would be more appropriate to conclude with a remark by the philosopher Ernst Bloch (1885–1977), paying tribute to the composer in 1923, in the 'spirit of utopia', as 'the greatest Chosen One of the dynamic, Luciferian spirit.'[214] Beethoven's music, passionate and spirited, stands for happiness that has yet to be achieved.

# Notes

*Sources of quotations (abbreviated list)*

*Briefe* (Letters): *Ludwig van Beethovens sämtliche Briefe*, ed Emerich Kastner. Reprint of the revised and considerably extended new edition by Dr Julius Kapp, Tutzing 1975. The number given in the notes refer to the numbering of the letters in this edition. However, the letters of Beethoven are not quoted from it, but by kind permission of the Beethoven Archiv and the publisher from the new critical complete edition of Beethoven's letters, published by Sieghard Brandenburg at Henle Verlag, Munich.

*Konversationshefte* (Conversation books): *Ludwig van Beethovens Konversationshefte*, 10 vols, eds. Karl-Heinz Köhler, Grita Herre and Dagmar Beck, Leipzig 1972–1993.

TDR: *Ludwig van Beethovens Leben*, Alexander Wheelock Thayer, edited and completed by Hermann Deiters, revised by Hugo Riemann. Leipzig, vol 1: 1917; vol 2: 1922; vol 3: 1923; vol 4: 1923; vol 5: 1908. In English: *Thayer's Life of Beethoven*. Rev and ed Elliot Forbes, 2nd Edition, Princeton, 1967

Wegeler-Ries: *Biographische Notizen über Ludwig van Beethoven*, Franz Gerhard Wegeler and Ferdinand Ries, Koblenz 1838. In English: *Remembering Beethoven: the Biographical Notes of Franz Wegeler and Ferdinand Ries*, trans Frederick Noonan, London, 1988

1 *Des Bonner Bäckermeisters Gottfried Fischer Aufzeichnungen über Beethovens Jugend*, ed Joseph Schmidt-Görg, Munich and Duisburg 1971, p. 61.

2 Ludwig Schiedermair, *Der junge Beethoven*, Leipzig 1925, p. 57.

3 *Cf* Sieghard Brandenburg, 'Beethovens politische Erfahrungen in Bonn', in *Beethoven. Zwischen Revolution und Restauration*, ed Helga Lühning and Sieghard Brandenburg, Bonn 1989, p. 5.

4 Fischer, as note 14, p. 32.

5 *Briefe*, no. 301.

6 *Konversationshefte*, vol 10, p. 297.

7 Fischer, as note 1, p. 52.

8 Fischer, as note 1, p. 57.

9 Schiedermair, as note 2, p. 130.

10 TDR, vol. 1, p. 43.

11 TDR, vol. 1, p. 45.

12 TDR, vol. 1, p. 430 f.

13 Fischer, as note 1, p. 51 f.

14 Fischer, as note 14, p. 40.

15 Wegeler-Ries, p. 10.

16 Irmgard Leux, *Christian Gotlob Neefe (1748–1798)*, Leipzig 1925, p. 198.

17 Brandenburg, as note 3, p. 11.

18  Schiedermair, as note 2, p. 161 f.

19  *Briefe*, no. 209.

20  Schiedemair, as note 2, p. 29.

21  TDR, vol. 1, p. 84.

22  TDR, vol. 1, p. 303.

23  Max Braubach (ed), *Die Stammbücher Beethovens und der Babette Koch*, Bonn 1995, p. 19.

24  *Briefe*, no. 52.

25  Wegeler-Ries, p. 33.

26  TDR, vol. 2, p 132.

27  Ludwig Nohl, *Beethoven. Nach den Schilderungen seiner Zeitgenossen*, Stuttgart 1877, p. 19 f.

28  Johann Wolfgang von Goethe, *Briefe*, vol. 3, ed. Bodo Morawe, Hamburg 1965, p. 200.

29  TDR, vol. 2, p. 175.

30  TDR, vol. 1, p. 356.

31  Robert Schumann, *Gesammelte Schriften über Musik und Musiker*, vol. 1, Leipzig 1871, p 331 f.

32  *Allgemeine Musikalische Zeitung*, year 5, April 1803, col. 489.

33  TDR, vol 2, p. 449.

34  Wegeler-Ries, p. 102.

35  Wegeler-Ries, p. 92.

36  Wegeler-Ries, p. 114.

37  Goethe to Zelter, 9 November 1829, quoted here from: *Briefwechsel Goethe-Zelter*, selected and ed. Werner Pfister, Zürich and Munich 1987, p 304.

38  Anton Schindler, *Ludwig van Beethoven*, ed Fritz Volbach, Münster, 1927, part 1, p. 39.

39  Johann Friedrich Reichardt, *Briefe, die Musik betreffend*, Leipzig 1976, p. 277, p. 272 f.

40  TDR, vol. 2, p. 238.

41  *Allgemeine Musikalische Zeitung*, year 8, January 1806, col. 237.

42  TDR, vol. 2, p. 37.

43  Otto Erich Deutsch, *Schubert. Die Erinnerungen seiner Freunde*, Leipzig 1957, p. 56.

44  Beethoven, *Werke*, section II, vol. 1, *Overtures and Wellington's Victory*, Munich 1974, p. 124.

45  TDR, vol. 3, p. 395.

46  TDR, vol. 3, p. 395.

47  TDR, vol. 3, p. 396.

48  TDR, vol. 3, p. 427.

49  Willy Hess, *Das Fidelio-Buch*, Winterthur 1986, p. 94.

50  *Briefe*, no. 43.

51  TDR, vol. 2, p. 142.

52  TDR, vol. 2, p. 143.

53  TDR, vol. 3, p. 123.

54  Barry Cooper (ed), *The Beethoven Compendium*, London, 1991, p69

55  *Cf* the list of subscribers for the Bridgetower concerts mentioned above, in TDR, vol. 2, p. 394.

56  From TDR, vol. 2, p. 445.

57  Martin Geck and Peter Schleuning, *'Geschrieben auf Bonaparte'. Beethovens 'Eroica': Revolution, Reaktion, Rezeption*, Reinbek bei Hamburg 1989, p. 225 ff.

58  *Konversationshefte*, vol. 2, p. 367.

59  Rudolf Klein, *Beethovenstätten in Österreich*, Vienna 1970; Kurt Smolee, *Wohnstätten Ludwig van Beethovens von 1792 bis zu seinem Tod*, Bonn 1970.

60  *Briefe*, no. 49.

61  *Briefe*, no. 52.

62  *Briefe*, no. 56.

63  Hedwig M. von Asow (ed.), *Ludwig van Beethoven. Heiligenstädter Testament*, facsimile, Vienna and Munich 1992, p. 10 ff.

64 *Briefe*, no. 65.

65 *Cf* Maynard Solomon, Beethoven, New York, 1977, revised edition, 1988, p. 154.

66 *Cf* Solomon, as note 65, p. 158.

67 Carl Czerny, *Erinnerungen aus meinem Leben*, ed Walter Kolneder, Strasbourg 1969, p. 14.

68 TDR, vol. 2, p. 566 f.

69 Wegeler-Ries, p. 98.

70 *Briefe*, no. 246.

71 TDR, vol. 4, p. 74.

72 Dagmar Busch-Weise, 'Beethovens Jugendtagebuch'. *Studien zur Musikwissenschaft*, vol. 25, Graz, Vienna, and Cologne 1962, pp. 77 and 84.

73 *Briefe*, no. 253.

74 Schindler, as note 38, par. 1, p. 241.

75 Harry Goldschmidt, *Um die Unsterbliche Geliebte*, Leipzig 1977, p. 60.

76 Joseph Schmidt-Görg, 'Wer war "die M." in einer wichtigen Aufzeichnung Beethovens', in *Beethoven-Jahrbuch* 1961/64, p. 75 ff.

77 Goldschmidt, as note 75, p. 19f *Cf* Sieghard Brandenburg (ed.), *Beethoven. Der Brief an die Unsterbliche Geliebte*, Bonn 1986.

78 Maynard Solomon, *Beethoven Essays*, Cambridge, Mass. and London 1988, p. 246.

79 Wegeler-Ries, p. 117.

80 Wegeler-Ries, p. 43.

81 *Briefe*, no. 17.

82 *Konversationshefte*, vol. 3, p. 157.

83 *Briefe*, no. 160.

84 La Mara (N. Lipsius), *Beethoven und die Brunsviks*, Leipzig 1920, p. 27 ff.

85 TDR, vol. 2, p. 307.

86 TDR, vol. 2, p. 307.

87 Marie-Elisabeth Tellenbach, *Beethoven und seine 'Unsterbliche Geliebte' Josephine Brunswick. Ihr Schicksal und der Einfluss auf Beethovens Werk*, Zürich 1983, p. 57; George R. Marek, *Ludwig van Beethoven. Das Leben eines Genies*, Munich 1970, p. 231.

88 Marek, as note 87, p. 234.

89 Tellenbach, as note 106, p. 60.

90 Joseph Schmidt-Görg (ed.), *Beethoven. Dreizehn unbekannte Briefe an Josephine Gräfin Deym geb. Brunsvik*, Bonn 1957, p. 20 f.

91 Schmidt-Görg, as note 90, p. 25 f.

92 Goldschmidt, as note 75, p. 145.

93 Schmidt-Görg, as note 90, p. 14.

94 *Briefe*, no. 188.

115 W. A. Thomas-San-Galli, *Ludwig van Beethoven*, Munich 1921, p. 261.

96 *Briefe*, no. 230.

97 *Briefe*, no. 242.

98 Tellenbach, as note 87, p. 125 ff.

99 Solomon, as note 65, p. 222 ff.

100 From Solomon, as note 65, p. 237.

101 Goethe, as note 28.

102 *Briefe*, no. 1272.

103 *Briefe*, no. 198.

104 *Briefe*, no. 100.

105 *Briefe*, nos. 36 and 37.

106 *Briefe*, nos. 294 and 306, also TDR, vol. 2, p. 115.

107 Wegeler-Ries, p. 116.

108 *Briefe*, no. 53.

109 Theodor Frimmel, *Beethoven-Handbuch*, vol. 1, Hildesheim and Wiesbaden 1968, p. 423.

110 TDR, vol. 3, p. 505.

111 *Briefe*, no. 245; sketchbook, Vienna A45, p. 25.

112 *Briefe*, no 900.

113 Bettina von Arnim, *Werke und Briefe*, vol. 2, ed. Gustav Konrad, Frechen 1959, p. 248.

114 Wilhelm Heinrich Wackenroder, *Werke und Briefe*, ed Ludwig Tieck, Heidelberg 1967, p. 204.

115 *Cf* among others Harry Goldschmidt, 'Vers und Strophe in Beethovens Instrumentalmusik', in: *Beethoven-Symposion Wien 1970*, Vienna 1971, pp. 97–120. Before Goldschmidt, Arnold Schering was the most notable scholar researching into this subject and offering interpretations.

116 Czerny, as note 67, p. 43.

117 Schindler, as note 38, Part 2, p. 221.

118 Amadeus Wendt, 'Gedanken über die neuere Tonkunst, und van Beethoven's Musik, namentlich dessen Fidelio', in: *Allgemeine Musikalische Zeitung*, year 17, 24 May 1815, col. 351.

119 Richard Wagner, *Sämtliche Schriften und Dichtungen*, Leipzig, n.d., 5th edition, vol. 3, p. 22 f.

120 Paul Bekker, *Die Sinfonie von Beethoven bis Mahler*, Berlin 1918, p. 15.

121 Wegeler-Ries, p. 78.

122 Wagner, as note 119, vol. 5, p. 169 f.

123 Carl Dahlhaus, 'Beethovens "Neuer Weg"', in: *Jahrbuch des Staatlichen Instituts für Musikforschung*, Berlin 1974, p. 54.

124 Cosima Wagner, *Die Tagebücher*, vol 2, ed. Martin Gregor-Dellin and Dietrich Mack, Munich and Zürich 1977, p. 568.

125 Schindler, as note 38, Part 1, p. 158.

126 *Cf* the passage under the heading 'Überwindung' in Hans-Heinrich Eggebrecht, *Zur Geschichte der Beethoven-Rezeption*, Laaber 1994, p. 71 ff See also Mechtild Fuchs, '*So pocht das Schicksal an die Pforte*' *Untersuchungen and Vorschläge zur Rezeption sinfonisher Musik des 19. Jahrhunderts*, Munich and Salzburg 1986.

127 Solomon, as note 78, p.

128 Harry Goldschmidt, *Beethoven – Werkeinführungen*, Leipzig 1975, p. 41 f.

129 *Cf* Peter Gülke, *Zur Neuausgabe der Sinfonie Nr. 5 von Ludwig van Beethoven. Werk und Edition*, Leipzig 1978, p. 53; also Martin Geck, 'Beethoven auf dem "neuen Weg". Zur Philosophie seiner V. Sinfonie', in: Renate Ulm (ed), *Die 9 Symphonien Beethovens*, Munich and Kassel 1994, p. 168 ff.

130 Friedrich Schiller, *Nationalausgabe der Werke*, vol. 20, Weimar 1962, p. 199.

131 Hilmar Frank, Joseph Anton Koch. *Der Schmadribachfall. Natur und Freiheit*, Frankfurt am Main 1995, p. 28.

132 Schiller, as note 130, p. 467.

133 Friedrich Hölderlin, *Sämtliche Werke*, vol. 2, ed. Friedrich Beissner, Stuttgart 1951, p. 147.

134 As note 111.

135 Hermann Kretzschmar, *Führer*

*durch den Konzertsaal.* 1. Abeteilung, vol. 1, Leipzig 41913, p. 234.

136 Carl Dahlhaus, 'Bemerkungen zu Beethovens 8. Symphonie', in: *Schweizerische Musikzeitung*, year 110, 1970, p. 209.

137 Leopold Schmidt, *Beethoven. Werke und Leben*, Berlin 1924, p. 215 f.

138 Wagner, as note 119, vol. 3, p. 94 f.

139 *Cf* Wolfgang Osthoff, 'Zum Vorstellungsgehalt des Allegretto in Beethovens 7. Symphonie', in: *Archiv für Musikwissenschaft*, year 34, 1977, p. 171 ff.

140 Elisabeth Eleonore Bauer, 'Beethoven – unser musikalischer Jean Paul', in: *Musikkonzepte 56. Beethoven: Analecta varia*, Munich 1987, p. 83 ff.

141 Jean Paul, *Vorschule der Ästhetik*, ed Norbert Miller, Munich 1974, pp. 132 and 129.

142 *Cf* Tellenbach, as note 87, p. 157.

143 Solomon, as note 78, p. 246.

144 Konversationshefte, vol. 1, pp. 211 and 235.

145 Albert Leitzmann (ed.), Ludwig van Beethoven. Berichte der Zeitgenossen, vol. 1, Leipzig 1921, p. 278 f.

146 Brandenburg, as note 77, p. 28.

147 *Briefe*, no. 581.

148 *Briefe*, no. 369.

149 TDR, vol. 3, p. 363.

150 TDR, vol. 3, p. 371.

151 Solomon, as note 65, p. 283.

152 Solomon, as note 78, p. 283; see also, as note 65, p. 284.

153 *Konversationshefte*, vol. 1, p. 266.

154 *Konversationshefte*, vol. 1, p. 267 f.

155 Solomon, as note 65, p. 108.

156 *Briefe*, no. 857.

157 *Briefe*, no. 1158.

158 Schindler, as note 38, part 1, p. 232.

159 *Briefe*, 1207.

160 Friedrich Rochlitz, *Für Freunde der Tonkunst*, vol. 4, Leipzig 1868, p. 229.

161 Solomon, as note 65, p. 333.

162 Rochlitz, as note 160, p. 235.

163 Rochlitz, as note 160, p. 231.

164 Leitzmann, as note 145, p. 185.

165 *Cf* the chapter 'Beethoven and his Nephew', in: Solomon, as note 65, p. 297 ff.

166 TDR, vol. 3, p. 518.

167 *Briefe*, no. 565.

168 Friedrich Kerst, (ed.), *Die Erinnerungen an Beethoven*, vol. 1, Stuttgart 1913, p. 200 f.

169 *Briefe*, no. 582.

170 *Briefe*, no. 600.

171 *Konversationshefte*, vol. 1, p. 311.

172 *Cf* Solomon, as note 65, p. 318.

173 Dagmar Weise, *Beethoven. Entwurf einer Denkschrift an das Alppellationsgericht*, Bonn 1953, p. 44.

174 *Konversationshefte*, vol. 10, p. 286.

175 *Konversationshefte*, vol. 10, p. 169.

176 *Konversationshefte*, vol. 10, p. 156.

177 *Briefe*, no. 493.

178 *Konversationshefte*, vol. 1, p. 210.

179 *Konversationshefte*, vol. 1, p. 339.

180 Kerst, as note 168, p. 263.

181 Solomon, as note 65, p. 398.

182 Wegeler-Ries, p. 146; *Briefe*, nos. 748 and 1044.

183 TDR, vol. 5, pp. 67–69.

184 Solomon, as note 65, p. 377.

185 Solomon, as note 65, p. 373.

186 *Aus Moscheles' Leben. Nach Briefen und Tageüchern seiner Frau*, vol. 1, Leipzig 1872, p. 153.

187 TDR, vol. 5, p. 492.

188 Carl Czerny, *Über den richtigen Vortrag der sämtlichen Beethoven'schen Klavierwerke*, ed Paul Badura-Skoda, Vienna 1963, p. 16.

189 Goldschmidt, as note 75, p. 280 ff., esp. p. 282.*Cf* also Jean and Brigitte Massin, *Recherche de Beethoven*, Paris 1970, p. 132 ff.

190 Wilhelm von Lenz, *Beethoven. Eine Kunst-Studie*, vol. 5, Hamburg 1860, p. 219.

191 *Briefe*, no. 1238.

192 Kurt von Fischer, 'Missa solemnis op. 123', in: Albrecht Riethmüller, Carl Dahlhaus and Alexander L. Ringer (eds.), *Beethoven. Interpretationen seiner Werke*, Laaber 1994, vol. 2, p. 248.

193 Gustav Nottebohm, *Zweite Beethoveniana*, Leipzig 1887, p. 163.

194 Richard Wagner, *Sämtliche Briefe*, vol 7, ed. Hans-Joachim Bauer and Johannes Forner, Leipzig 1988, p. 204.

195 From a copy in the Beethoven House. Cf also: Nottebohm, as note 193, p 189 ff; TDR, vol. 5, p. 27 f.; Sieghard Brandenburg, 'Die Skizzen zur Neunten Symphonie', in: Harry Goldschmidt (ed.), *Zu Beethoven*, vol. 2, Berlin 1984, p. 88 ff.,

196 Thomas Mann, *Doktor Faustus*. In: *Gesammelte Werke*, vol. 6, Frankfurt am Main, 1960, p. 634.

197 Manfred Hermann Schmid, 'Streichquartett a-Moll op. 132', in: Riethmüller et al., as note 192, vol. 2, p. 337 (citing Philip Radcliffe).

198 Wagner, as note 119, p. 96 f.

199 Theodor W. Adorno, *Beethoven, Philosophie der Musik*, Frankfurt am Main, 1993, p. 267.

200 Franz Grillparzer, 'Rede am Grabe Beethovens', in: *Sämtliche Werke*, vol. 14, Prosaschriften II, Vienna 1925, p. 45 f.

201 Sebastian Hensel, *Die Familie Mendelssohn 1729–1847 nach Briefen und Tagebüchern*, vol. 1, Berlin 1911, p. 213 f.

202 Deutsch, as note 43, p. 109.

203 Max Kalbeck, *Brahms*, vol. 1, 1, Berlin 1908, p. 165.

204 Josef Bohuslav Foerster, *Der Pilger. Erinnerungen eines Musikers*, Prague 1955, p. 408.

205 Franz Liszt, *Gesammelte Schriften*, vol 1, Leipzig 1880, p. 163.

206 E. T. A. Hoffmann, 'Beethovens Instrumentalmusik', in: *Musikalische Dichtungen und Aufsätze*, Stuttgart 1922, p. 305.

207 Robert Schumann, *Tagebücher*, vol 1, ed Georg Eismann, Basel and Frankfurt am Main 1971, p. 97.

208 Eggebrecht, as note 126, p. 56.

209 Pierre Boulez, *Wille und Zufall. Gespräche mit Célestin Deliège und Hans Mayer*, Stuttgard and Zürich 1977, p. 149.

210 Romain Rolland, *Beethovens Meisterjahre. Von der Eroica zur Appassionata*, German edition tr. Th. Mutzenbecher, Berlin 1952,

p. 7. Following quotation, p. 6.

211 Martin Geck and Peter Schleuning, *'Geschrieben auf Bonaparte. Beethovens 'Eroica': Revolution, Reaktion, Rezeption*, Reinbek bei Hamburg, 1989, p. 242. The following quotations, p. 284 f. (Bülow), p. 300 (Vetter), p. 344 (Rosenberg), p. 346 (Ney), p. 322 (Eisler and the labour movement), p. 322 (Wiegand).

212 Hugo von Hofmannsthal in his 'Rede auf Beethoven', 1920, quoted from Geck-Schleuning, as note 211, p. 328.

213 Richard Dehmel, 'Jesus und Psyche. Phantasie bei Klinger', in: *Gesammelte Werke*, vol. 1, Berlin 1913, p. 190.

214 Ernst Bloch, *Geist der Utopie*. Revised new edition of the second version of 1923, Frankfurt am Main 1964, p. 88.

# Chronology

| Year | Age | Life |
|------|-----|------|
| 1770 | | Ludwig van Beethoven baptised in Bonn (parents: Johann van Beethoven and Maria Magdalena, *née* Keverich). |
| 1773 | 3 | 24 December, death of his grandfather. |
| 1774 | 4 | 8 April: baptism of his brother Kaspar Karl. Beethoven's father begins teaching him music. |
| 1775 | 5 | 2 October: baptism of his brother Nikolaus Johann |
| 1778 | 8 | 26 March, first appearance at an Academy concert in Cologne. |
| 1781 | 11 | Begins taking lessons from Christian Gottlob Neefe. Travels to Holland with his mother. |
| 1782 | 12 | Makes friends with Franz Wegeler and the aristocratic Breuning family. Publication of Beethoven's Dressler Variations (WoO 63). |
| 1783 | 13 | Beethoven becomes a salaried member of the Bonn Hofkapelle. Publication of 3 Kurfürsten Sonatas WoO 47. |
| 1784 | 14 | Election of Archduke Maximilian Franz as Elector of Cologne. Beethoven is appointed deputy court organist. |
| 1785 | 15 | Composes 3 Piano Quartets WoO 36. |
| 1786 | 16 | Composes Trio for Flute, Bassoon and Piano WoO 37. |
| 1787 | 17 | April: Briefly studies with Mozart in Vienna. Early July: returns home. 17 July: death of his mother. |
| 1788 | 18 | Count Waldstein arrives in Bonn. |

| Year | History | Culture |
|------|---------|---------|
| 1770 | Boston Massacre. | Edmund Burke, *Thoughts on Present Discontents.* |
| 1773 | Boston Tea Party. | C W Gluck, *Iphigénie en Aulide.* Oliver Goldsmith, *She Stoops to Conquer.* J W Goethe, *Goetz von Berlichingen.* |
| 1774 | Louis XVI becomes king. British parliament passes Coercive Acts against Boston and Massachusetts. Joseph Priestley discovers oxygen. | Goethe, *The Sorrows of Young Werther.* |
| 1778 | France supports America in revolution; Britain declares war on France. Evangelical revival: Methodism in Britain; Pietism in Germany and Switzerland; and the Great Awakening in America. | Wolfgang Amadeus Mozart, *Paris* symphony. La Scala opera house opens in Milan. |
| 1781 | Joseph II of Austria declares himself 'Enlightened Despot' in effort to modernise Holy Roman Empire. Charles Cornwallis surrenders at Yorktown; end of American revolution. William Herschel discovers Uranus. | Mozart, *Idomeneo.* F Schiller, *Die Räuber.* Immanuel Kant, *Critique of Pure Reason.* Henry Fuseli, *The Nightmare.* |
| 1782 | James Watt patents double-acting rotary steam engine. | Mozart, *Entführang aus dem Serail.* |
| 1783 | Treaty of Versailles between Britain, France, Spain and US. Montgolfier brothers invent hot-air balloon. | |
| 1784 | Treaty of Constantinople: Russia annexes Crimea. | P A C Beaumarchais, *Le Mariage de Figaro.* |
| 1786 | Henry Cavendish discovers that water is a compound rather than an element. Bonn University inauguration | |
| 1787 | US constitution is signed. | Mozart, *Don Giovanni.* Schiller, *Don Carlos.* |

| Year | Age | Life |
|------|-----|------|
| 1789 | 19 | Upon his father's retirement, Beethoven assumes guardianship of his brothers. Plays viola in a number of Mozart operas at the Court Opera, including *Figaro* and *Don Giovanni*. |
| 1790 | 20 | Meets Count Waldstein. Haydn and Salomon arrive in Bonn. |
| 1791 | 21 | Travels to Bad Mergentheim with the Bonn Hofkapelle. |
| 1792 | 22 | November: Beethoven's second journey to Vienna. Composition of the String Trio Op 3. 18 December, death of his father. Begins study with Haydn. |
| 1793 | 23 | Studies with Johann Schenk. Visits Prince Esterházy in Eisenstadt with Haydn. Publishes 'Se Vuol Ballare Variations' on *Figaro*. |
| 1794 | 24 | Begins to study counterpoint with Albrechtsberger, when Haydn leaves for London. His brother Carl arrives in Vienna. |
| 1795 | 25 | Spring: finishes study with Albrechtsberger. 29 March: first public appearance in Vienna. Publication of the Piano Trio Op 1. December: performs Piano Concerto at one of Haydn's concerts. |
| 1796 | 26 | February: travels to Prague, Dresden, Leipzig and Berlin, where he writes the Op 5 Sonatas for the cellist Jean-Louis Duport. Meets the king of Prussia and Prince Louis Ferdinand. 23 November: concert in Pressburg. Composition of Adelaide Op 46. |
| 1797 | 27 | Schuppanzigh premières the Quintet Op 16 in its Piano Quartet version |
| 1798 | 28 | Beethoven's hearing begins to fail. Composition of the Sonate pathétique Op 13. March: performs the Sonatas Op 12 with Schuppanzigh. |
| 1799 | 29 | Begins composing the Op 18 Quartets and the 1st Symphony. Begins study with Anton Salieri. |

| Year | History | Culture |
|------|---------|---------|
| 1789 | French Revolution. George Washington inaugurated as US president. Antoine Lavoisier establishes modern chemistry. | Mozart, *Cosi fan tutte*. William Blake, *Songs of Innocence*. Jeremy Bentham, *Introduction to the Principles of Morals and Legislation*. |
| 1790 | Leopold II becomes Holy Roman Emperor. | Burke, *Reflections on the Revolution in France*. Kant, *Critique of Judgement*. |
| 1791 | Counter-revolutionaries organise military invasion of France from Germany. US Congress meets in Philadelphia; selects site of District of Colombia. P D Toussaint-L'Ouverture leads slave revolt in Haiti. | Mozart, *The Magic Flute*. Mozart dies. James Boswell, *Life of Johnson*. Thomas Paine, *The Rights of Man*. |
| 1792 | French Republic proclaimed. Battle of Valmy. French troops invade Mainz | C J Rouget de Lisle, 'La Marseillaise'. Mary Wollstonecraft, *A Vindication of the Rights of Women*. |
| 1793 | Louis XVI and Marie Antoinette executed. Reign of Terror under Robespierre in France. Second partition of Poland. | J L David, *The Death of Marat*. The Louvre becomes a public art gallery. |
| 1794 | Robespierre executed. Eli Whitney patents cotton-gin in US. | Blake, *Songs of Experience*. Erasmus Darwin, *Zoonomia*. Xavier De Maistre, *Voyage autour de ma chambre*. |
| 1795 | Methodists formally split from the Church of England. Third partition of Poland. Directory government in France. Whiskey Rebellion in US. Hydraulic press invented in England. | Goethe, *Wilhelm Meisters Lehrjahre*. |
| 1796 | Edward Jenner discovers smallpox vaccine. | |
| 1797 | John Adams inaugurated as US president. Treaty of Campo Formio. France creates Cisalpine Republic and annexes left bank of Rhine. French Ambassador Bernadotte arrives in Vienna | Cherubini, *Medea*. |
| 1798 | France invades Egypt. Alois Senefelder invents lithography. | Samuel Taylor Coleridge and William Wordsworth, *Lyrical Ballads*. T R Malthus, *An Essay on the Principle of Population*. |

| Year | Age | Life |
|------|-----|------|
| 1800 | 30 | Composition of the String Quartets Op 18. 2 April: gives his own first Academy, performing the First Symphony, Septet Op 20 and the First Piano Concerto. April–May: performs Horn Sonata Op 17, with Johann Stich (Punto) in Vienna and Budapest. Czerny and Ferdinand Ries become Beethoven's pupils. Accepts pension from Prince Lichnowsky. |
| 1801 | 31 | 28 March: première of the ballet *The Creatures of Prometheus*. Letters to Wegeler and Karl Amenda on the subject of his deafness. |
| 1802 | 32 | Anton Reicha reunited with Beethoven. October: writes the Heiligenstadt Testament. November: dispute with Artaria over publication of the Op 29 Quintet. |
| 1803 | 33 | Beethoven continues dispute with Artaria over the Op 29 Quintet. 5 April: Academy with the Second Symphony, Third Piano Concerto and the Oratorio Christ on the *Mount of Olives*. George Bridgetower arrives in Vienna. The Kreutzer Sonata Op 47 completed and performed. Works on the Eroica. Commissioned by Schikaneder to write an opera. |
| 1804 | 34 | First private performances of the Eroica. Works on his opera *Fidelio*. July: Ries plays the Third Concerto with Beethoven conducting. |
| 1805 | 35 | 7 April: first public performance of the Eroica. July: meeting with Cherubini. 20 November: first performance of *Fidelio* (1st version). |
| 1806 | 36 | 29 March: first performance of 2nd version of *Fidelio*. 23 December: première of the Violin Concerto. Completes the Rasumovsky Quartets, Op 59. October: violent quarrel with Lichnowsky; destroys his bust of the Prince. |
| 1807 | 37 | Composition of the Mass Op 86 for Prince Esterházy, première on 13 September. Subscription concerts in Prince Lobkowitz's palace, with works including the Fourth Symphony, Fourth Piano Concerto, *Coriolan* overture. |
| 1808 | 38 | March: Beethoven suffers serious infection, nearly resulting in the loss of a finger. Asked by King Jérôme to go to Kassel as his Kapellmeister. 22 December: Academy with première of the Fifth and Sixth Symphonies, the Choral Fantasia Op 80, and parts of the Mass Op 86. |
| 1809 | 39 | February: agreement on a long-term pension with Princes Lobkowitz and Kinsky as well as Archduke Rudolph. Composition of the Fifth Piano Concerto and the String Quartet Op 74, 'The Harp'. |

| Year | History | Culture |
|------|---------|---------|
| 1800 | Battle of Marengo. Alessandro Volta makes first battery. | Cherubini, *The Water-Carrier*. J G Fichte, *The Vocation of Man*. |
| 1801 | Thomas Jefferson inaugurated as US president. Irish Act of Union. Napoleon and Pope Pius VII sign concordat. Alexander I becomes tsar of Russia. | Joseph Haydn, *The Seasons*. F R Chateaubriand, *Atala*. |
| 1802 | France annexes Piedmont. Treaty of Amiens. First steamship built. | Chateaubriand, *Le Génie du christianisme*. |
| 1803 | Louisiana Purchase. Britain declares war on France. | |
| 1804 | Pope crowns Napoleon emperor. Haiti becomes independent. Civil Code created in France. | Blake, *Jerusalem*. |
| 1805 | Battle of Austerlitz. Battle of Trafalgar. Mehemet Ali becomes Pasha of Egypt. | Wordsworth, *The Prelude*. J M W Turner, *Shipwreck*. |
| 1806 | Holy Roman Empire ends. Battle of Jena. Death of Prussian Prince Louis Ferdinand. Battle of Auerstädt. Napoleon forms Confederation of Rhine. | Jean-Dominique Ingres, *Napoleon on the Imperial Throne*. |
| 1807 | Jérôme Bonaparte installed as king of Westphalia, Bernadotte as King of Sweden. Colombian independence movement begins. Robert Fulton invents paddle steamer. | G W Hegel, *Phenomenology of Mind*. David, *Coronation of Napoleon*. |
| 1808 | Peninsular War (until 1814). J L Gay-Lussac discovers laws of gas expansion. | Goethe, *Faust* (Part I), |
| 1809 | James Madison inaugurated as US president. France occupies Papal States. | |

| Year | Age | Life |
|------|-----|------|
| 1810 | 40 | Plans to marry Therese Malfatti. 15 June: first performance of the music for *Egmont*. 168 arrangements of British folksongs by 1822. |
| 1811 | 41 | Works on the Seventh and Eighth Symphonies and the Piano Trio Op 97 |
| 1812 | 42 | 9 February: premières of the incidental music to *The Ruins of Athens* Op 113 and *King Stephen* Op 117 in Pest. Summer, meets Goethe at the spa resort of Teplitz and writes letter to the Immortal Beloved. Death of Prince Kinsky. December: Pierre Rode and Archduke Rudolph premiere the Sonata Op 96. |
| 1813 | 43 | 8 December: première of the battle tone-poem *Wellington's Victory* and the Seventh Symphony. |
| 1814 | 44 | 27 February: Academy at which the Eighth Symphony is performed. 23 May: revises *Fidelio* (3rd version). Death of Prince Lichnowsky. December: the Razoumovsky palace and instrument collection burns down. |
| 1815 | 45 | Concerts for the Congress of Vienna. Death of his brother Kaspar Karl. Becomes guardian of his nephew Karl. 25 December: première of Calm Sea and Prosperous Voyage Op 112. Beethoven appeals to remove Johanna rights of custody of Karl. Writes Polonaise Op 89 for the Tsarina, to embarrass Alexander I into paying for the Op 30 Sonatas. |
| 1816 | 46 | Landrecht tribunal awards Beethoven custody of Karl, to whom Czerny begins to give piano lessons. Song cycle *An die ferne Geliebte* Op 98. Death of Prince Lobkowitz. |
| 1817 | 47 | Beethoven invited to London. Fugue for String Quartet Op 137 composed. |
| 1818 | 48 | Piano Sonata Op 106. December: Karl runs away from school. |
| 1819 | 49 | Is now completely deaf; begins using the conversation books. Starts work on the *Missa solemnis*. October: Beethoven tries to buy a house, unsuccessfully. |
| 1820 | 50 | March: Archduke Rudolph enthroned as Archbishop of Olmütz. The custody case is decided in Beethoven's favour. Composition of the Piano Sonata Op 109. |

| Year | History | Culture |
|------|---------|---------|
| 1810 | Fulani empire in Sokoto. | |
| 1811 | King George III's 'mad-business'; Prince Regent installed in Britain. Luddite riots against machines. | Jane Austen, *Sense and Sensibility*. |
| 1812 | France invades Russia; forced to withdraw by end of year. US declares war on Britain. | J and W Grimm, *Fairy Tales*. Hegel, *Logic*. |
| 1813 | Battle of Leipzig. | Austen, *Pride and Prejudice*. Lord Byron, *Childe Harold's Pilgrimage*. |
| 1814 | Napoleon abdicates. Congress of Vienna convened (until 1815). Louis XVIII restored as king of France. Ferdinand VII restored as king of Spain. Jesuits restored. | Franz Schubert, *Gretchen am Spinnrade*. Francisco de Goya, *The Disasters of War* (until 1814). |
| 1815 | Hundred Days in France. Battle of Waterloo. Napoleon exiled to St Helena. German states form confederation. Holy Alliance in central and eastern Europe. | |
| 1816 | Congress of Tucumán. René Laënnec invents monaural stethoscope. | G Rossini, *The Barber of Seville*. Austen, *Emma*. Coleridge, 'Kubla Khan'. |
| 1818 | Shaka forms Zulu kingdom. Chile declares independence. | Austen, *Persuasion*. Mary Shelley, *Frankenstein*. Prado museum opens in Madrid. |
| 1819 | Stamford Raffles founds Singapore. US purchases Florida from Spain. Simón Bolívar forms Gran Colombia. | Schubert, *Trout Quintet*. John Keats, 'Ode to a Nightingale'. Arthur Schopenhauer, *World as Will and Idea*. Théodore Géricault, *Raft of the Medusa*. |
| 1820 | George IV becomes king of Britain. Missouri Compromise. | Walter Scott, *Ivanhoe*. P B Shelley, *Prometheus Unbound*. Venus de Milo is discovered. |

| Year | Age | Life |
|------|-----|------|
| 1821 | 51 | March: Josephine Deym-Brunsvik-Stackelberg dies. Beethoven is ill with jaundice. Works on the Piano Sonata Op 110. |
| 1822 | 52 | April: Rossini visits Beethoven in Vienna. Première of the overture *The Consecration of the House* Op 124 for the opening of the Josephstadt Theatre on 3 October. Works on the Ninth Symphony. Anton Schindler becomes Beethoven's assistant. |
| 1823 | 53 | April: Beethoven attends recital given by the 11-year-old Liszt. Completes the *Missa solemnis* and the Diabelli Variations Op 120. |
| 1824 | 54 | 6 April, première of the *Missa solemnis* in St Petersburg. 7 May, Academy with première of the Ninth Symphony and parts of the *Missa solemnis*. Composition of the String Quartet Op 127 |
| 1825 | 55 | Böhm gives successful performance of Op 127 after Schuppanzigh's unsuccessful premiere. March: British première of the Ninth Symphony. September: meets Kuhlau. |
| 1826 | 56 | January: completes Quartet Op 130. 21 March: performance of the String Quartet Op 130 by Schuppanzigh. 30 July: suicide attempt of Beethoven's nephew. Stays at his brother's estate at Gneixendorf. Last composition, a new finale to Op 130. Plans a tenth symphony. Falls severely ill. |
| 1827 | 57 | January: Karl leaves for military service. Long final illness. 26 March: dies after many years of suffering from chronic liver trouble. Buried on 29 March. June: Death of Stephan von Breuning. November: auction of Beethoven's effects. |

| Year | History | Culture |
|------|---------|---------|
| 1821 | Famine in Ireland. Insurrection in Piedmont. Greek war of independence begins. | Thomas De Quincey, *Confessions of an English Opium-Eater*. Hegel, *Philosophy of Right*. John Constable, *The Hay Wain*. |
| 1822 | Liberia founded for freed US slaves. Greece declares independence. Brazil declares independence. J F Champollion deciphers Egyptian hieroglyphics using the Rosetta Stone. | Alexander Pushkin, *Eugene Onegin* (until 1832). |
| 1823 | Monroe Doctrine. First Anglo-Burmese war. | |
| 1824 | Charles X becomes king of France. | Byron, *Don Juan*. National Gallery founded in London. |
| 1825 | Nicholas I becomes tsar of Russia. Decembrist revolt suppressed in Russia. Japan confirms laws of European exclusion. | Schubert, *Death and the Maiden* quartet. Pushkin, *Boris Godunov*. |
| 1826 | Seku Ahmadu conquers Timbuktu. | James Fenimore Cooper, *Last of the Mohicans*. |
| 1827 | Battle of Navarino. Duke of Wellington becomes PM of Britain. | Schubert, *Die Winterreise*. |

# List of Works

Dates given are dates of composition.
Numbers in square brackets after the titles of the works are page references to discussion of the work in the text.

## Instrumental works

### SYMPHONIES

Symphony No 1 in C Op 21 (1799–1800) [pp. 74–5]
Symphony No 2 in D Op 36 (1801–02) [ p. 25]
Symphony No 3 in E flat 'Eroica' Op 55 (1803–04) [pp. 75–81]
Symphony No 4 in B flat Op 60 (1806) [p. 26]
Symphony No 5 in C minor Op 67 (1807–08) [pp. 78–81]
Symphony No 6 in F 'Pastoral' Op 68 (1807–08) [pp. 81–5]
Symphony No 7 in A Op 92 (1811–12) [pp. 85–6]
Symphony No 8 in F Op 93 (1811–12) [pp. 86–8]
Symphony No 9 in D minor Op 125 (1822–24) [pp. 118–20]

### OVERTURES AND *WELLINGTON'S VICTORY*

Overture to *Die Geschöpfe des Prometheus (The Creatures of Prometheus)*
    Op 43 (1800–01) [p. 28]
Overture *Leonore* I Op 138 (1808)
Overture *Leonore* II (1805)
Overture *Leonore* III (1806)
Overture to Collin's *Coriolan (Coriolanus)* Op 62 (1807) [p. 26]
Overture to Goethe's *Egmont* Op 84 (1809–10) [p. 31]
Overture to *Die Ruinen von Athen (The Ruins of Athens)* Op 113 (1811)
Overture to *König Stephan (King Stephen)* Op 117 (1811)
*Wellingtons Sieg oder Die Schlacht bei Vittoria; Schlachtensinfonie (Wellington's*
    *Victory or The Battle of Vittoria; Battle Symphony)* Op 91 (1813) [pp. 31–2]
Overture *Fidelio* (1814)

Overture *Namensfeier (The Name Day)* Op 115 (1814–15) [p. 33]

Overture *Die Weihe des Hauses (The Consecration of the House)* Op 124 (1822)
[pp. 106–8]

BALLETS AND INCIDENTAL MUSIC

*Die Geschöpfe des Prometheus (The Creatures of Prometheus)*, ballet, Op 43
(1800–01) [pp. 75–6]

Incidental music to Goethe's *Egmont* Op 84 (1809–10) [p. 31]

Incidental music to *Die Ruinen von Athen (The Ruins of Athens)* Op 113
(1811) [p. 31]

Incidental music to *König Stephan (King Stephen)* Op 117 (1811) [p. 31]

Incidental music to *Leonore Prohaska* WoO 96 (1815)

CONCERTOS

Piano Concerto in E flat WoO 4 (1784)

Piano Concerto No 1 in C Op 15 (ca. 1795–96, 1798) [p. 25]

Piano Concerto No 2 in B flat Op 19 (1794–95, 1798)

Piano Concerto No 3 in C minor Op 37 (1800) [p. 23]

Piano Concerto No 4 in G Op 58 (1805–06) [p. 26]

Piano Concerto No 5 in E flat Op 73 (1809) [p. 27]

Violin Concerto in D Op 61 (1806)

Triple Concerto for piano, violin and cello in C Op 56 (1803–04) [p. 36]

CHAMBER MUSIC · VARIOUS GROUPINGS

Octet for wind instruments in E flat Op 103 (1792)

Quintet for Piano and Wind, or version for Piano Quartet Op 16 (1799) [p. xii]

Septet in E flat Op 20 (1799–1800) [p. 25]

Sextet for wind instruments in E flat Op 71 (1796)

Sextet for string quartet and 2 horns in E flat Op 81b (1794 or 1795)

String Quintet in E flat Op 4 (arranged from the Octet for wind Op 103)
(1795–96)

String Quintet in C Op 29 (1800–01) [p. 34]

Fugue for string quintet in D Op 137 (1817)

Three Quartets for piano, violin, viola and cello in E flat, D, and C WoO 36
(1785) [p. 10]

## STRING QUARTETS

Six String Quartets Nos 1–6 in F, G, D, C minor, A, and B flat Op 18
(1798–1800) [p. 57]
Three String Quartets Nos 7–9 in F, E minor, and C ('Razumovsky
Quartets') Op 59 (1805–06) [p. 24]
String Quartet No 10 in E flat ('Harp Quartet') Op 74 (1809)
String Quartet No 11 in F minor Op 95 (1810)
String Quartet No 12 in E flat Op 127 (1824–25) [p. vii]
String Quartet No 13 in B flat Op 130 (1825–26) [p. 169]
String Quartet No 14 in C sharp minor Op 131 (1826) [pp. 123–4]
String Quartet No 15 in A minor Op 132 (1825) [pp. 122–3]
Grosse Fuge for String Quartet in B flat Op 133 (1825) [p. 109]
String Quartet No 16 in F Op 135 (1826) [p. 110]

## TRIOS

Piano Trio in E flat WoO 38 (1790–91)
Three Piano Trios in E flat, G and C minor Op 1 (1793–94) [p. 20]
Trio for clarinet, cello and piano Op 11 (1797)  [p. 19]
Two Piano Trios in D ('Ghost Trio') and E flat Op 70 (1808)
Piano Trio in B flat ('Archduke Trio') Op 97 (1811) [p. 46]
Allegretto for piano trio in B flat WoO 39 (1812)
String Trio in E flat Op 3 (1792)
Serenade for string trio in D Op 8 (1796–97)
Three String Trios in G, D and C minor Op 9 (1796–98)
Serenade for flute, violin and viola in D Op 25 (1795–96)
Trio for 2 oboes and English horn in C Op 87 (1794)

## SONATAS FOR TWO INSTRUMENTS

Three Sonatas for piano and violin in D, A and E flat Op 12
(1797–98) [p. 26]
Sonata for piano and violin in A minor Op 23 (1800)
Sonata for piano and violin in F ('Spring') Op 24 (1800–01)
Three Sonatas for piano and violin in A, C minor and G Op 30 (1802)
[p. xi]
Sonata for piano and violin in A ('Kreutzer') Op 47 (1802–03) [p. x–xi]

Sonata for piano and violin in G Op 96 (1812)

Two Sonatas for piano and cello in F and G minor Op 5 (1796)

Sonata for piano and cello in A Op 69 (1807)

Two Sonatas for piano and cello in C and D Op 102 (1815) [pp. 114–5]

Sonata for piano and horn in F Op 17 (1800)

PIANO SONATAS

Three Sonatas in E flat, F minor and D ('Kurfürstensonaten') WoO 47
    (1782–83) [p. 10]

Three Sonatas nos. 1–3 in F minor, A and C Op 2 (1795) [p. 20]

Sonata No 4 in E flat Op 7 (1796–97)

Three Sonatas Nos 5–7 in C minor, F and D Op 10 (1796–98)

Sonata No 8 in C minor ('Pathétique') Op 13 (1798–99) [pp. 69–71]

Two Sonatas Nos. 9–10 in E and G Op 14 (1798–99)

Sonata No 11 in B flat Op 22 (1799–1800)

Sonata No 12 in A flat Op 26 (1800–01)

Two Sonatas (*quasi una fantasia*) Nos. 13–14 in E flat and C sharp minor
    ('Moonlight Sonata') Op 27 (1801) [p. 55]

Sonata No 15 in D Op 28 (1801)

Three Sonatas Nos 16–18 in G, D minor and E flat Op 31 (1801–02)
    [pp. 71–3]

Two Sonatas Nos 19–20 in G minor and G Op 49 (1798, 1796)

Sonata No 21 in C ('Waldstein Sonata') Op 53 (1803–04)

Sonata No 22 in F Op 54 (1804)

Sonata No 23 in F minor ('Appassionata') Op 57 (1804–05) [p. 72]

Sonata No 24 in F sharp Op 78 (1809)

Sonatina No 25 in G Op 79 ((1809)

Sonata No 26 in E flat ('Les adieux') Op 81a (1809–10) [p. 69]

Sonata No 27 in E minor Op 90 (1814)

Sonata No 28 in A Op 101 (1816) [p. 105]

Sonata No 29 in B flat ('Hammerklavier Sonata') Op 106 (1817–18) [p. 114]

Sonata No 30 in E Op 109 (1820) [p. 105]

Sonata No 31 in A flat Op 110 (1821) [p. 114]

Sonata No 32 in C minor Op 111 (1821–22) [p. 105]

Six Variations on an Original Theme in F Op 34 (1802) [p. 43]

Fifteen Variations on an Original theme in E flat ('Eroica Variations')
Op 35 (1802)

Six Variations on an Original Theme in D Op 76 (1809)

Thirty-three Variations on a Waltz by A. Diabelli in C Op 120
(1822–23) [p. 61]

Rondo a capriccio in G ('Rage Over a Lost Penny') Op 129 (between 1795
and 1798)

Seven Bagatelles Op 33 (1802)

Bagatelle in A minor ('Für Elise') WoO 59 (1810)

Eleven Bagatelles Op 119 (1820–22)

Six Bagatelles Op 126 (1823–24) [p. 105]

# Vocal works

### OPERA

*Fidelio oder Die Eheliche Liebe (Leonore); Fidelio or Married Love (Leonore)* Op 72
(1st version with *Leonore* Overture II 1804–05; 2nd version with
*Leonore* Overture III 1805–06; 3rd version with *Fidelio* Overture 1814)
[pp. 29–31]

### MASSES

Mass in C Op 86 (1807) [p. 26]

*Missa solemnis* (Solemn Mass) in D Op 123 (1819–23) [pp. 116–7]

### ORATORIOS, CANTATAS AND SONGS WITH ORCHESTRA

Cantata on the Death of Emperor Joseph II WoO 87 (1790) [p. 15]

Cantata on the Elevation of Leopold II to the Imperial Dignity WoO 88
(1790)

Scena and Aria *Ah perfido!* For soprano and orchestra Op 65 (1796) [p. 26]

'Bundeslied' for two soloists and three choral parts with wind instrument
accompaniment (setting of words by Goethe) Op 122 (1797–1822)

*Christus am Ölberge* (*Christ on the Mount of Olives*) (oratorio) Op 85
(1803) [p. 25]

Fantasia for piano, chorus and orchestra Op 80 (1808) [p. 26]

Elegiac Song for four voices and string quartet accompaniment Op 118
(1814)

Cantata *Der glorreiche Augenblick* (*The Glorious Moment*) Op 136 (1814) [p. 103]

'Germania', closing song from G F Tretischke's Singspiel *Die gute Nachricht*
(*Good News*) for bass with chorus and orchestra WoO 94 (1814) [p. 33]

'Ihr weisen Gründer' ('Ye wise founders'), chorus with orchestra on the
subject of the allied princes WoO 95 (1814)

'Meeresstille und glückliche Fahrt' (Calm Sea and Prosperous Voyage)
Op 112 (1814–15) [p. 33]


LIEDER AND SONGS WITH PIANO ACCOMPANIMENT

Eight Lieder Op 52 (1790–99)

'Adelaide' (Matthison) Op 46 (1795–96)

'Ich liebe dich' ('I love you') (K F Herrosee) WoO 123 (1797)

'Der Kuss' (The Kiss) (C F Weisse) Op 128 (1798)

Six Lieder to texts by C F Gellert Op 48 (1798–1802)

Six Songs Op 75 (1809)

Three Songs to poems by Goethe Op 83 (1810)

'An die Hoffnung' (To Hope) (C. A. Tiedge): 1st version Op 32 (1805); 2nd
version Op 94 (1813–15) [p. 58]

*An die ferne Geliebte* (*To the Distant Beloved*), song cycle to words by Alois
Jeitteles Op 98 (1816) [p. 105]

Arrangements of over 200 Scottish, Irish and Welsh folksongs, and a
smaller number of Spanish, Russian, Polish, Hungarian, Scandinavian,
Italian, French, and English folksongs for one or more voices Piano
trio, and in sets Op 108 (1815–16) and WoO 152–156 (1810–22)

# Select Discography

This is a selection of recordings of Beethoven's music that may safely be recommended.

SYMPHONIES

Sir John Eliot Gardiner (cond)
  Orchestre Révolutionnaire et Romantique
  Archiv (Deutsche Gramophon) Production 439 900-2AH5
Herbert von Karajan (cond)
  Berlin Philharmonic Orchestra
  Deutsche Gramophon 439 200-2

PIANO CONCERTOS

Wilhelm Kempf (piano); Ferdinand Leitner (cond)
  Berlin Philharmonic Orchestra
  Deutsche Gramophon 427 237-2GX3
Alfred Brendel (piano); Sir Simon Rattle (cond)
  Vienna Philharmonic Orchestra
  Philips 462 781-2PH3

VIOLIN CONCERTO

David Oistrakh; André Cluytens
  French National Radio Orchestra.
  EMI

STRING QUARTETS (COMPLETE CYCLES)

Smetana Quartet
  Supraphon
Guarneri Quartet. Philips
Budapest Quartet. Sony MH2K62870
              MH2K62873

## PIANO TRIOS

Beaux Arts Trio
  Philips The Early Years 438 948-2PM3

## STRING TRIOS

Leopold String Trio
  Hyperion CDA67253 and CDA67254

## VIOLIN SONATAS

Gideon Kremer (violin); Martha Argerich (piano).
  Deutsche Gramophon DG 652-2GH (Sonatas Nos 6–8)
Peter Sheppard Skærved (violin); Aaron Shorr (piano)
  Metier

## CELLO SONATAS

Mischa Maisky (cello); Martha Argerich (piano)
  Deutsche Gramophon 431 801-2 and 437 514-2

## PIANO SONATAS

Stephen Kovacevich
  EMI CDC5 56586-2 (Nos 8–11)
  EMI CDC5 55226-2 (Nos 16–18)
  EMI CDC7 54896-2 (Nos 21, 24, 31)

## MISSA SOLEMNIS

Sir Colin Davis (cond)
  London Symphony Orchestra
  Philips 438 362-2

## LIEDER

Dietrich Fischer-Dieskau; Jörg Demus
  Deutsche Gramophon

# Further Reading

There is a vast range of literature on Beethoven, much of it in German. We have selected a few titles that offer a good next step for the interested reader and are published in English. We have also included a few important books still only available in German.

## GENERAL GUIDES

Barry Cooper (ed), *The Beethoven Compendium: A Guide to Beethoven's Life and Music*, London, 1991 is an excellent store of information on Beethoven's life, historical background and music.

## LIFE: LETTERS, 'CONVERSATION BOOKS' AND MEMOIRS

E. Anderson (ed and trans), *The Letters of Beethoven*, 3 vols, Macmillan London, 1961, offers a good selection of the letters in English.

Karl-Heinz Köhler, Grita Herre and Dagmar Beck (eds), *Ludwig van Beethovens Konversationshefte* [Conversation books], complete edition in 10 vols, Leipzig, 1972–1993

Gerhard von Breuning, *Memories of Beethoven: From the House of the Black-Robed Spaniards*, ed Maynard Solomon, trans Henry Mins and Maynard Solomon, Cambridge, 1992

Franz Gerhard Wegeler and Ferdinand Ries, *Remembering Beethoven: the Biographical Notes of Franz Wegeler and Ferdinand Ries*, trans Frederick Noonan, London 1988

## LIFE: OTHER BIOGRAPHIES

Biographers of Beethoven have always faced the problems associated with such a legendary figure. His life was being mythologized or distorted even during his lifetime (not least by himself) and he attracted several unreliable biographers or memoirists. In the second half of the 19th century the American musicologist Alexander Wheelock Thayer devoted his life's work to writing the first comprehensive account of the composer's life, which was initially published in a German version by Hermann Deiters. Deiters supervised the publication of the first three volumes of *Beethoven* up to the time of his death in 1907. Hugo Riemann, one of the founding fathers of German musicology, edited the missing volumes 4 and 5, working from proofs and manuscripts, and then revised the first three volumes, adding discussions of the separate works. Hugo Riemann's five-volume version was finished in 1917.

In 1964, Princeton University Press published the revision of Henry Edward Krehbiel's 1921 translation of Thayer-Deiters-Riemann, by the Harvard professor Elliot Forbes. Rather than rewrite the text, Forbes chose to overlay it with commentary, illuminating obscure passages, and suggesting alternatives where mistakes have occurred. This is now seen as an authoritative version and is widely accepted in Germany and Austria.

Alexander Wheelock Thayer, *Thayer's Life of Beethoven*, rev and ed Elliot Forbes, 2nd Edition, Princeton, 1967

Maynard Solomon, *Beethoven*, New York 1977, 2nd edition New York 1998. This is the best account of the composer's life now available. It may be overloaded with psychoanalytical theories, but is interestingly written and well abreast of Beethoven research.

H C Robbins Landon, *Beethoven: His Life, Work and World*, London, 1970, 2nd edition 1992. This volume is distinguished from many other similar works in that it contains many large-scale illustrations.

Russell Martin, *Beethoven's Hair: An Extraordinary Historical Odyssey and a Musical Mystery Solved*, London, 2000. This is a fascinatingly oblique glance into the most arcane corner of musicology, where reliquary, 20th-century political history, forensic science and library theft combine to give a surprisingly moving account of the last days of Beethoven and, believe it or not, the Nazi occupation of Denmark.

## THE MUSIC

Theodor W. Adorno, *The Philosophy of Music*, ed Rolf Tiedemann, tr Edmund Jephcott, Cambridge, 1998

Scott Burnham and Michael P Steinberg (eds), *Beethoven and His World*, Princeton NJ, 2000. A collection of essays addressing Beethoven's compositions and their cultural context, ranging from how Beethoven chose his pianos to an investigation of the impact of his funeral in Vienna.

Leon Plantínga, *Beethoven's Concertos: History, Style, Performance*, New York, 1999

Robert Winter and Robert Martin (eds), *The Beethoven Quartet Companion*, Berkeley, Los Angeles and London, 1994

## HISTORICAL CONTEXT

Tia De Nora, *Beethoven and the Construction of Genius: The Musical Politics of Vienna, 1792–1803*, California, 1995

Alexander Ringer (ed), *Music and Society – The Early Romantic Era*, London, 1990. A lively purview of music in Beethoven's world, city by city – very entertaining and informative.

# About the Author

Martin Geck, born in 1936, studied musicology, theology and philosophy in Münster, Berlin and Kiel. He took his doctorate in 1962 and in 1966 became founding editor of the Gesamtausgabe of the works of Richard Wagner. He wrote a number of musicological textbooks, became an assistant lecturer in 1974, and was appointed full professor of musicology at Dortmund University in 1976.

He has edited and written many books, articles and entries in encyclopaedic works on the history of German music in the 17th, 18th and 19th centuries, concentrating in particular on the work of Schütz, Buxtehude, Bruhns, Bach, Beethoven, E. T. A. Hoffmann, Mendelssohn-Bartholdy and Wagner. He is co-editor of the catalogue of the works of Richard Wagner. His standard work *Von Beethoven bis Mahler. Die Musik des deutschen Idealismus* (*From Beethoven to Mahler. The music of German idealism*) appeared in 1993.

At present his research concentrates mainly on Johann Sebastian Bach. His full-scale study *Bach: Leben und Werk* (*Bach: Life and Work*) was published in Germany in 2000 and is being translated into English. His biography of Bach is also published in the *Life&Times* series.

The author would like to thank Dr Helga Lühning of the Beethoven Archive in Bonn for her expert advice.

# Picture Sources

The author and publishers wish to express their thanks to the following sources of illustrative material and/or permission to reproduce it. They will make proper acknowledgements in future editions in the event that any omissions have occurred.

Beethoven Museum, Bonn: pp. 39, 48, 55, 60, 61, 111; The British Museum: pp. viii, ix; Lebrecht Music Collection: pp. 1, 6, 7, 8, 9, 12, 16, 20, 30, 36, 37, 41, 43, 50, 65, 66, 72, 75, 77, 84, 89, 90, 96, 99, 107, 108, 116, 121, 124, 127, 130, 133, 134

# Index